Praise for *Walk with Me*

Bill Mowry writes with winsome clarity about a subject that is near to the heart of God and invites us into the ways of Jesus Christ. No other topic reflects more fully the life and purposes of Jesus than His focus on helping everyday people walk with God and reflect His character. Bill makes it doable for all of us, people in busy lives and in a culture that tries to pull us away from meaning and relationship.

DOUG NUENKE
US President of The Navigators

After seeing the dead end of church life driven by constant programming and new gimmicks, I believe American Christians are beginning to rediscover the beautiful simplicity of Jesus' method of disciplemaking. *Walk with Me* is a practical guide for that journey. With decades of hands-on experience, Bill Mowry offers winsome advice and helpful stories about learning to make disciples in everyday life. Whether you're a church leader looking to lead cultural change, or a churchgoer who is ready to get in the game and start learning how to make disciples, this book is for you!

MATT REYNOLDS
President, Spirit and Truth Ministries

If you're interested in helping others become more Christ-centered, it would make sense to listen to someone with a life of experience in disciplemaking. As a friend of Bill Mowry, I have watched his life for the past thirty years, and these pages contain much of his wisdom. I suggest you read *Walk with Me*!

WILLIAM B. MALARKEY
Professor Emeritus of Internal Medicine, The Ohio State University

In a Christian culture where disciplemaking has been relegated to professionals, Bill Mowry has revealed from Scripture that making disciples is something every follower of Jesus can do and should do! Bill is not only an author but a practitioner I have observed firsthand in the context of our local church. I invite you to walk with him on the journey of learning your role in making disciples.

BRENT MILLER
Lead Pastor, Linworth Baptist Church, Worth

As an experienced disciplemaker, I found this book to be one that provides both clarity and simplicity to a process that can easily become complex and intimidating. Bill Mowry does well in unpacking the simple relational dynamics that make a disciplemaking relationship so transformational. If you are looking to grow as a disciplemaker, this is one of the best books available to make it achievable.

PATTI DAMIANI
Woman's Leader and Speaker
Relational Wisdom Coach

This is an extremely practical book on helping "ordinary people" like you and me make disciples. Bill Mowry takes a simple step-by-step approach to lifetime disciplemaking. Reading this book will transform your thoughts from "I am not capable" to "I'm empowered by God to be able!" Definitely a must-read!

DEBI ZAAS
The Navigators Life & Leadership Coaching Codirector

Walk with Me is the classic readable Bill Mowry on the wonder-filled, intentional journey of interpersonal disciplemaking. Written from the tireless suburban missionary practitioner himself, the guide is a perfect gift to a new generation of difference-making millennials who will be inspired to place Jesus' essential ways at the center of their lifestyle . . . for the glory of God and the good of their neighbor.

CHIP WEIANT
Senior Fellow, BBB National Center for Character Ethics
Board Member, Ohio Governor's Office of Faith-Based and Community Initiatives

Bill's book is a pleasure to read. It is packed with practical insight on how to begin, or mature, as a disciplemaker. Bill's engaging writing style and easy-to-relate-to stories helpfully illustrate the principles he is teaching, which are sensitive to contemporary cultural challenges. Bill draws on a lifetime of experience in making disciples, showing how it is accessible and uniquely rewarding, and offers this to the church. It is a gift whose rarity makes it even more precious. I found myself taking notes.

ADAM DODDS
Senior Pastor, Elim Church, Dunedin, New Zealand

Walk with Me is the fruit of Bill's decades-long practice, study, and teaching about the art of disciplemaking. Bill provides thought-provoking and practical insights into the secrets of life-changing relationships. This book makes disciplemaking simple and doable for every follower of Jesus, whether a beginner or a veteran disciple.

TYLER FLYNN
Former pastor and Executive Director of Mission Columbus

If you want to grow in your ability and understanding of disciplemaking, *Walk with Me* by Bill Mowry is your book. It can be easy to get overwhelmed by the call of Christ to "make disciples," but this book helps us keep things simple, practical, and intentional. Anyone looking to grow in the area of disciplemaking should read this book.

JAMIE STRICKLAND
Pastor of Discipleship Ministries, West Highland Church, Hamilton, ON, Canada

Years ago, Bill invited me to walk with him while he walked with Jesus. I wasn't sure what I was getting into then, but now I can see how far Bill has brought me—and how far I've been able to bring my church with his help and coaching. My life has changed; now God is working in my church to change the lives of others, and all because Bill asked me to walk with him years ago. This book will teach you the same, simple principles of disciplemaking that Bill taught and showed me.

ERIC WATERS
St. John Lutheran Church, Boerne, TX

Several months ago, I set a personal goal to walk ten thousand steps a day. With an aging body, I needed the exercise to stay in shape physically. It's now a regular habit that I miss if I can't fit it in. What if Christians today started inviting people to "walk with them as they walk with Jesus" as a nonnegotiable part of their daily routine? *Walk with Me* explains how to do that in accessible, easy-to-understand language. Imagine how much our troubled world would change if we Christ followers were committed to the metaphorical equivalent of 10,000 steps a day habit for this kind of discipleship walk?

MARY SCHALLER
Coauthor of *The 9 Arts of Spiritual Conversations*

If you're looking for a practical, doable, and biblical way to disciple a friend, then this book is for you. It is a field manual for a person-to-person, heart-to-heart, Holy Spirit–guided micro ministry of disciplemaking.

JOE VALENTINO
Campus Pastor, Upper Arlington Lutheran Church, Upper Arlington, OH

I have no one I would rather talk to about life and mission than Bill Mowry. After you read this book, you will see why. Bill has the ability to make difficult subjects interesting and simple. This approach to disciplemaking is what the body of Christ needs today.

HOWARD VAN CLEAVE
InterVarsity Graduate and Faculty Ministry, The Ohio State University

In our hectic culture and church world, we have made the Great Commission complex, expensive, and inaccessible to the everyday person. *Walk with Me* counters this state of affairs with the simple biblical metaphor of "walking." *Walk with Me* is a practical book that will help pastors, church leaders, and everyday disciples begin taking their first steps to help others follow Jesus as His disciples.

DANE ALLPHIN
National Lead, The Navigators Church Ministries

WALK WITH ME

SIMPLE PRINCIPLES FOR EVERYDAY DISCIPLEMAKING

BILL MOWRY

MOODY PUBLISHERS

CHICAGO

Edited by Pamela J. Pugh
Interior design: Brandi Davis
Cover design: Erik M. Peterson
Cover illustration of street sign copyright © 2018 by -VICTOR- / iStock (1030917706).
Cover illustration of landscape copyright © 2020 by BLUE COLLECTORS / Stocksy (3204511).
Cover illustration of silhouettes copyright © 2014 by Rawpixel / iStock (496852117).
All rights reserved for the photos above.
Author photo: Carla Shadwick

Library of Congress Cataloging-in-Publication Data

Names: Mowry, Bill, 1950- author.
Title: Walk with me : simple principles for everyday disciplemaking / Bill Mowry.
Description: Chicago : Moody Publishers, [2021] | Includes bibliographical references. | Summary: "Have we overcomplicated, oversystematized, and overformalized making disciples? When our hearts are changed by Christ, it's natural that we should want to help others come to know Him too. And while Scripture clearly sets forth how to do so, modern Western society has formalized, professionalized, and systematized disciplemaking to a point that it seems too complicated to practice. What happened to the simple, heart-to-heart ministries of the New Testament? In Walk with Me, you'll return to the essential biblical practices that help people grow as Christ-followers in simple, slow, and deep ways. Learn how you can connect with your neighbors, coworkers, or anyone you want to reach with the gospel in ways that are relational and Spirit-led"-- Provided by publisher.
Identifiers: LCCN 2020035373 (print) | LCCN 2020035374 (ebook) | ISBN 9780802420299 (paperback) | ISBN 9780802498922 (ebook)
Subjects: LCSH: Witness bearing (Christianity) | Discipling (Christianity)
Classification: LCC BV4520 .M648 2021 (print) | LCC BV4520 (ebook) | DDC 248/.5--dc23
LC record available at https://lccn.loc.gov/2020035373
LC ebook record available at https://lccn.loc.gov/2020035374

Originally delivered by fleets of horse-drawn wagons, the affordable paperbacks from D. L. Moody's publishing house resourced the church and served everyday people. Now, after more than 125 years of publishing and ministry, Moody Publishers' mission remains the same—even if our delivery systems have changed a bit. For more information on other books (and resources) created from a biblical perspective, go to www.moodypublishers.com or write to:

Moody Publishers
820 N. LaSalle Boulevard
Chicago, IL 60610

3 5 7 9 10 8 6 4 2

Printed in the United States of America

This book is dedicated to my parents, Bill and Daisy Mowry. They set the example of loving God and loving their neighbors, making disciples and sharing their faith, living in "the quiet" (see 1 Thessalonians 4:11–12) of a small rural town.

CONTENTS

AN INVITATION

I hate to run.

Maybe it's the memories of pounding mile after mile when I ran track in high school. Today, I walk for exercise and have two types of walking. One is done in a community fitness center on a track and is very fast. The other is done with my wife, Peggy, and it's done slowly.

I'm a solitary walker on the fitness center track, but there are plenty of others in couples or groups along the way. I have given some of them names as I pass them on my workout.

First are the lovebirds. This Asian American couple laughs and holds hands as they walk. Another pair are the senior strollers—an older couple who walk like they're strolling down a country lane. No workout gear for them; they show up in street clothes. Finally, there's the "pack." This group of three or four women march around the track talking about their families, their jobs, and their husbands—laughing and having fun.

What do they all have in common? Walking is a relational activity. I hear snippets of personal stories, fears, heartaches, and laughter as I pass them. The same happens when Peggy and I walk together. The goal is not to see how fast we can go or how much territory we can cover (unlike my time in the gym), but it's about the conversations we have. Walking together encourages heart-to-heart conversations.

The Bible frequently uses the word "walk" to describe our relationship with God. For example, Genesis 6:9 says that "Noah walked with God." This verb "walk" communicates that Noah's life with Him is, as Eugene Peterson puts it, "a lifelong, companionable, conversational friendship with God."[1]

I think the image of walking with friends is a wonderful picture for disciplemaking.

The words "disciple" and "disciplemaking" are probably not new to you. The church today is experiencing a wake-up call to this ministry. Why? When we spend time in the Gospels, we quickly discover Jesus' commitment to make disciples. In fact, the theme of making disciples runs throughout the New Testament. Author Dallas Willard writes that "the word 'disciple' occurs 269 times in the New Testament. . . . The New Testament is a book about disciples, by disciples, and for disciples of Jesus Christ."[2] A disciple is someone committed to living Jesus' way of life and embracing His mission. Making disciples was high on Jesus' priority list, and He wants it to be a high priority for us (more about this later).

Second, pastors and ministry leaders are discovering a lack of depth in people's lives. Too often, churches can be, as the saying goes, "a mile wide and an inch deep." As researcher George Barna documents, "believers are more likely to court dimensions of life other than spirituality as the springboard to success and meaning."[3] Something more is needed to turn the tide of superficiality, and that "something more" is discipleship. We must move, and help others move, from a life of superficiality and spiritual infancy to one of maturity in Christ and living on mission for Christ. Disciples live lives of maturity and mission.

This awakening to discipleship is driving leaders to seek the holy grail of disciplemaking—the perfect curriculum, the motivational program, or a dynamic staff person—that will turn a church or ministry into an intentional disciplemaking one. This often means spending a lot of money and time in organization, purchasing materials, and salaries. Is there another way?

What if there was an approach to disciplemaking that did not require an expensive curriculum, a paid professional, or a state-of-the-art website? What if there was a way to make disciples that was simple enough for everyone to practice? What if there was a process integrated to life, even life in our busy, multitasking world?

I'm writing to demonstrate that disciplemaking can be as simple as inviting people to walk with me as I walk with Jesus. I'm inviting you to learn and practice a disciplemaking lifestyle that is a walk between friends. This walk practices some simple principles that make disciplemaking accessible to anyone who loves God and desires to help others follow Jesus. Disciplemaking should not be reserved for ministry professionals or a select spiritual few. Disciplemaking should be practiced by everyday believers in the everyday routines of where we live, work, play, or study.

Disciplemaking starts when we intentionally invite people to walk with us.

When we invite people to walk with us in the way of Jesus, we're inviting them to a heart-to-heart relationship done slowly with the Holy Spirit's help, which takes us and others to a greater depth in Christ. I'm inviting you to learn how to help others follow Jesus in ways that are heart-to-heart, simple, slow, deep, and on mission.

Walks are adventures. We never know what we might see, hear, or feel as we walk with God and with one another. When you invite people to walk with you as you walk with Jesus, you're entering a God-filled adventure. Are you ready to start?

START WALKING

*Walking is something nondramatic, rhythmic—
it consists of steady, repeated actions you can keep
up in a sustained way for a long time.*

TIMOTHY KELLER

I started walking fifty years ago. I took my first steps when I met Ed in college.

I was a student on a mission when I started college in 1968. My heroes were in the radical political left, my mission was social justice and ending the Vietnam War, my life values were defined by the rock-and-roll culture, and my first love was a girl named Peggy. Then I met Ed.

Ed lived across the hall from me in the freshman dorm. Two things quickly jumped out about Ed. One, he had a twin brother who was his roommate. Two, these brothers owned a black 1947 Fleetwood Cadillac that had once been a hearse. What guy wouldn't want to be their friend and ride in this car!

We became friends around the shared issues of college life— classes, girls, and music. But this friendship was different. Ed claimed to be a Christian. I had never met anyone my age who centered their life around their faith. I was skeptical of him at first, but Ed whet my appetite for Jesus through his example and over lots of late-night discussions.

Without going into all the details, the Lord lovingly drew me to Himself and I became a Christ follower in my second year of college. Ed was a big influence in this process. I found a new hero in Jesus, a new mission around the gospel, a new culture shaped by the Bible, and a new love for God.

While I sat in his dorm room excitedly describing my new-found faith, Ed issued a life-changing invitation. "Want to meet in the study lounge tomorrow and read the Bible together?"

He invited me to walk with him as he walked with Jesus. Little did I know that this simple invitation would mark my life for eternity.

I took up Ed's invitation and met with him in the study lounge the next day. We did the things that friends naturally do—laughed, debated, shared our dreams—but we did something more: we read the Bible together. In the weeks ahead, Ed taught me how to pray, study the Bible, and share my faith. He passed on the value of honesty, the value of love, and more important, what it meant to walk with God.

I wasn't a project to Ed. He invited me into a relationship—a friendship with him and with Jesus. Ed started me on a lifelong walk of loving God and giving my life to others. It all began with an invitation. A college student named Ed, just a regular guy, modeled inviting someone to "walk with me as I walk with Jesus."

WALKING IS BIBLICAL

Ed's invitation to read the Bible pointed to something bigger. His invitation to walk with him as he walked with Jesus reflected a biblical pattern that began with the Lord Himself.

Do you know when some of the disciples were first introduced to Jesus? It takes place in John 1:35–39:[1]

> The next day again John was standing with two of his disciples, and he looked at Jesus as he walked by and said, "Behold, the Lamb of God!" The two disciples heard him say this, and they followed Jesus. Jesus turned and saw them following and said to them, "What are you seeking?" And they said to him, "Rabbi" (which means Teacher), "where are you staying?" He said to them, "Come and you will see."

John the Baptist's disciples were intrigued by his declaration of Jesus as the "Lamb of God." They cautiously trailed this new rabbi, hesitant about beginning a conversation. When Jesus saw them, He turned to face them, first asking a question and then issuing an invitation.

In Judaism, the student would typically take the initiative to find a teacher or rabbi. These two men were already in the hunt. After all, they were following the Baptist. But this new rabbi turned the tables, taking the initiative to recruit them.[2] Jesus started the conversation, opening the door of relationship and inviting them in.

One commentator describes the encounter in this way:

> It was not mere curiosity which made these two ask this
> question ["where are you staying?"]. What they meant
> was that they did not wish to speak to Jesus only on the
> road, in passing, as chance acquaintances might stop
> and exchange a few words. They wished to linger long
> with him.[3]

How did the two disciples answer? They asked Jesus where
He was staying. How did Jesus respond? He gave an invitation:
"Come and see." This rabbi was asking them to join Him in
something more than just a chance conversation. He was inviting
them to be with Him "not as an acquaintance in passing, but as a
friend in their own homes."[4]

Nearly a year and a half later, Jesus formally invited a larger
group of twelve friends to live life and ministry "with him" (Mark
3:13–14). He relationally invested in these men. This is the heart
of disciplemaking—intentionally inviting people into a relationship, not a classroom, a lecture series, or a prepackaged curriculum. Disciplemaking is a "with Him" enterprise, an intentional,
up-close, and personal relationship and walk together.

The apostle Paul followed Jesus' pattern. Paul is never without
friends in the book of Acts. Consider how he recruited Timothy.
Their walk together begins in Lystra when Paul invites Timothy
to walk with him, as we read in Acts 16:1.

In rapid succession, they visit churches (v. 5), change direction
under the Spirit's guidance (v. 10), lead a wealthy woman to Christ
(v. 14), exorcise a demon from a slave girl (v. 18), cause a riot (v. 22),

are beaten in public (v. 23), and end up in prison (v. 24). Timothy's probably wondering, *Why did I ever say yes to joining this guy?*

Now scroll to the end of Paul's life. As he's waiting for his trial, Paul writes to Timothy, reminding him how he has "followed my teaching, my conduct, my aim in life" (2 Tim. 3:10). Timothy knew from an up-close-and-personal experience what Paul's conduct, aim, and teaching were. Those few nights in Philippi alone showed Timothy all he needed to know about this man! Paul had invited Timothy to walk with him as he walked with Jesus.

For most of us, this invitation to walk is not quite as dramatic as Paul's to Timothy. It's probably more like mine and my friend Todd.

My story doesn't end with Ed's invitation to read the Bible. Ed's example taught me that I could invite friends to walk with me as I walked with Jesus. I began praying for one friend to join me on this walk. Todd was that answer to prayer.

"LET'S MEET IN THE STUDY LOUNGE AND READ THE BIBLE TOGETHER."

Todd was another friend from the dorm. Like me, he initially had no use for God but began to notice the God-changes in friends around him. They were all talking about Jesus! Through a variety of divinely ordained circumstances, Todd placed his faith in Christ. When he told me his story, I extended a simple invitation. "Let's meet in the study lounge and read the Bible together."

I found out later that I wasn't the only one meeting to read the Bible in that study lounge. Ed was being helped by the local Navigator staff member Chuck; they were also meeting in that study lounge for a discipleship appointment. Chuck was helping Ed, who helped me, who helped Todd. This is 2 Timothy 2:2 in action—Paul to Timothy to faithful people who would "teach others also." What a simple vision to impact the world: disciples making disciples who make disciples who make disciples.

Ed's invitation to read the Bible gave me a life purpose and opened up a vocation when I joined The Navigators as a full-time staff person in my mid-twenties. I was captivated and committed to this vision of disciples making disciples. The Navigators's mission is "to know Christ, make Him known, and help others do the same."[5]

As a Navigator staff, I've been making disciples in a variety of settings—from undergraduates to professors, from doctors to dentists, from business leaders to church leaders. My life has been one of inviting people to come and walk with me as I walk with Jesus.

Over the past five decades, I've learned some lessons about disciplemaking: what it means to intentionally invite people to walk with me on this journey of following Christ. This invitation is an intentional one. I'm inviting others to follow Jesus with me, purposefully joining together to learn how to live for Christ in all of life. How do you do this? It's all about a walk and some simple principles.

WALKING ISN'T COMPLICATED

In the early 1970s the hot book on disciplemaking was *The Master Plan of Evangelism* by Robert Coleman. It was the "hot" book because there was little else in Christian bookstores on disciplemaking, and Coleman did a masterful job of describing this ministry of Jesus. How things have changed today!

Today, our bookshelves sag from the weight of disciplemaking books (including the books that I have written!). An entire industry has emerged, packaging disciplemaking curriculums, formulas, and franchises for building disciplemaking ministries and churches.

We have compiled disciplemaking agendas, checklists, and how-to manuals. I can appreciate the developers' thoroughness and commitment, but I often wonder if we have made something simple—an intentional relationship among a few people—too complex. I know the danger of this because I once did that very thing.

As a former practitioner of complexity, I had a neatly defined disciplemaking program. In fact, I had pages and file folders filled with outlines, studies, and goals for disciplemaking. I was sure of myself, believing that if people would only follow my step-by-step approach, then making disciples would naturally happen.

I was so intent on the program that I often missed the relationship with people. I accomplished my goals but failed to engage people's hearts. I forgot the relational example of Ed and instead settled for a program.

Now, programs are useful tools in disciplemaking, but they're often overrated when it comes to transformation. Time and experience have taught me that God's program is to use Spirit-led people who employ biblical principles in heart-to-heart ways. In other words, we invite people to walk with us as we walk with Jesus. To disciple people this way means simplifying and de-professionalizing disciplemaking.

By simplifying, I mean stripping the practice down to its bare essentials—allowing disciplemaking to be accessible for many. When we de-professionalize the Great Commission, we remove it from the hands of ministry professionals and turn it over to every-day people. To do this, we must circle back to some fundamental biblical principles and practices. We need to see disciplemaking as an invitation to follow Christ together, inviting people to walk with us in this life with Jesus.

WALKING IS FOR EVERYONE

Do you feel a little intimidated by inviting people to walk with you as you walk with Jesus? If you do, then you're qualified to extend this invitation to others. Jesus doesn't want skilled experts or know-it-alls but people who extend the invitation with humility. *Our* inability becomes an opportunity for the Lord to show *His* ability. We invite people to walk with us because we focus not on ourselves but on the person we're inviting them to follow: the Lord Jesus.

If you feel inadequate and have doubts about disciplemaking, then you're in good company. The initial group of men Jesus commissioned to go and make disciples of all nations also had reservations.

Let's consider Matthew 28:16–20. We call this the Great Commission passage because in this account Jesus commissions the eleven, sending them on a mission to disciple others.

> Now the eleven disciples went to Galilee, to the mountain to which Jesus had directed them. And when they saw him they worshiped him, but some doubted. And Jesus came and said to them, "All authority in heaven and on earth has been given to me. Go therefore and make disciples of all nations . . . teaching them to

observe all that I have commanded you. And behold, I
am with you always, to the end of the age."

What do you first notice? The disciples faithfully show up to
a prearranged meeting place and engage in spontaneous worship.
You would think that everything was going great, but did you
notice the author's brief observation, "but some doubted"?

The text is silent about what their doubts were. This gathering
was post-resurrection, so I don't think they were doubting who
this Man was. They knew it was the Master risen from the dead.
I wonder if the doubt was about their upcoming mission. Jesus
had stressed from day one of their time together that He had a
plan in mind for them (Matt. 4:19; Mark 3:14). I wonder if the
solemnity of the occasion raised some doubts about whether they
could carry out the Lord's mission.

Maybe the eleven were thinking: "Can
I do this?" "Can God use me?" "What
about my past failures?" We all ask these
questions. Given their responses during
His arrest, trial, and crucifixion, I can see
how they would be filled with doubts.
How could Jesus entrust a mission to a
group of cowards who fled at His arrest,
denied Him at His life crisis, and hid in
locked rooms after His death?

Our life circumstances may not be as
dramatic as the original disciples, but if
we're honest, we all have doubts about whether we're qualified to
invite someone to walk with us. We wonder if we can be obedient

I PICTURE JESUS GIVING A BLANK CHECK TO HIS FOLLOWERS— "WHATEVER YOU NEED TO FULFILL MY MISSION I WILL GIVE TO YOU"— NO MATTER WHO WE ARE OR WHERE WE ARE!

to His command. However, one action does stand out with the eleven: whatever their doubts, they showed up . . . and so can we!

How does Jesus counter these doubts? He gave this small group of friends two assurances in Matthew 28. First, He promised that His authority would be with them no matter where they go (v. 18). Second, He promised to be present with them no matter where they go (v. 20).

I picture Jesus giving a blank check to His followers— "whatever you need to fulfill My mission I will give to you"—no matter who we are or where we are! He is asking people to show up with all their doubts, fears, and insecurities to be empowered by Him for the task. I think most of us reading this book can qualify for this. His assurance moves disciplemaking from the practice of the spiritual "giants" to the ordinary person.

The twentieth-century author Francis Schaeffer wrote a wonderful book called *No Little People*. What a great title! There are no little people in God's eyes. In fact, our Lord seems to delight in using "little" people, ordinary, live-next-door, regular kind of people. These are people like the eleven disciples, and they are people like my friend Glenn.

Glenn was a junior in college when I invited him to a campus Bible study. He was a thoughtful, reserved guy, and underneath his quiet demeanor was a person of character. He had a heart for God and faithfully showed up for the Bible study and took steps to apply what he learned. He was also a music major, a detail that's important to know for this story.

After his graduation, I lost track of Glenn for quite some time. In a casual conversation at a training seminar one day around twenty-five years later, my colleague Dina mentioned how her daughter had been discipled by her music teacher. I inquired who the teacher was, and her answer surprised me. It turned out to be Glenn!

Here was a music teacher at a public school, inviting a group of students to read the Bible with him outside of school time. Glenn had showed up in his high school to do the Great Commission. In the everyday routine of high school life and music instruction, he invited people to walk with him as he walked with Jesus.

WALKING IS PROGRESSIVE— ONE STEP AT A TIME

My friend Terry coined a new name for a mental trap that he often found himself in: omni-competency. Omni-competency tells us that we have to be competent—fully skilled—in everything we do. Sometimes beginning disciplemakers (and even seasoned ones) can fall into the trap of omni-competency.

We think spiritual perfection is required before we can invite others to walk with us as we walk with Jesus. Here's some good news: the Scriptures do not demand perfection, but the Lord does expect practice and progress. Paul exhorts the young leader Timothy to "*Practice* these things, immerse yourself in them, so that all may see your *progress*" (1 Tim. 4:15).

"Practicing" the faith does not mean achieving perfection but putting into action what we know. Author Ken Boa describes practitioners as those "not following biblical laws to check a box but doing practical things to get close to God—like we do with anyone we want to be close to."[6]

With practice comes "progression." We're experiencing spiritual transformation, the process of seeing our lives change "from one degree of glory to another" (2 Cor. 3:18). People who know us should be able to observe signs of spiritual change and growth. Sometimes my progress feels like I'm taking two steps forward and one step back, but the important thing is to keep moving forward.

Paul saw this tension in his own life:

> Not that I have already obtained this or am already perfect, but I press on to make it my own, because Christ Jesus has made me his own. Brothers, I do not consider that I have made it my own. But one thing I do: forgetting what lies behind and straining forward to what lies ahead, I press on toward the goal for the prize of the upward call of God in Christ Jesus.
> —*Philippians 3:12–14*

The picture of "pressing" toward the goal is the word used of a racer going hard for the tape at the finish line. "Here is the runner in the games, 'extended' in every fibre of his being."[7] He or she forgets all that was behind them in an effort to reach the tape before anyone else. Perfection is not required, but effort and progress is. Like Paul, we press on, making progress, not achieving perfection.

Here's another encouraging principle: we can take people as far as we've come in our own walk with Jesus. Not all of us have walked the entire road of the Christian life. We have "practiced" the faith up to a certain mile marker, but there is still more road to travel. We can't invite people to a road we haven't experienced, but we can invite them to journey as far as we've come.

Pastor and author Brennan Manning writes that when we pretend to have walked a route unfamiliar to us, "we become unconvicted and unpersuasive travel agents handing out brochures to places we have never visited."[8] We can only invite people to walk as far as we have walked, and no further. So when I reach a point in the road where the path is unfamiliar, I invite someone who has already walked the path to join us. The church is full of other practitioners.

My calling to vocational ministry is both advantageous and limiting. For example, I've never had to deal with the rigors of office life or the challenge of living in the competitive corporate world. When meeting with Dwight, I discovered that my experience in helping him with work issues was limited. He was asking questions such as, "As a supervisor, I want to care for people, but are there professional limits, especially with women?" and "I want to share my faith, but I don't want this to feel like the 'boss' talking."

Disciplemaking does not mean that I have all the answers, that I have to be omni-competent. I connected Dwight with Nick, a mature believer who was also in middle management. Nick has walked this path before, and I trusted the advice he would give Dwight.

This is what the body of Christ is all about when it comes to disciplemaking. Too often, we think the Christian life is a singles match, but in reality it's a team sport. We don't have to walk alone with people; we have the resources of a local church or ministry available to us.

I believe the Lord wants to use "little" people—those everyday, ordinary, life-in-the-routine people. These people may be "little," but they're practitioners of the faith, seeking to live out among others what they believe. Maybe you're one of these little people, pressing on to know Jesus, not obtaining perfection but making progress. This walk, this practice, is never a solitary journey because we walk with the authority of Jesus and in the presence of Jesus, and we do it with friends (what we call the "church"). Like the apostles, we show up, trusting God to use our lives.

WALKING IS NOT FOLLOWING

Let's make a distinction in terms. We cannot ask people to *follow* us, but we can invite them to *walk* with us. There's a difference between following and walking. Jesus called people to "follow" Him (Matt. 4:19). Following Jesus as a disciple means the unconditional surrender of one's whole life, a life "bound to Jesus and to do God's will."[9] We do not invite people to surrender their wills to us. Only Jesus can make this request.

Walking is a relationship between equals (Jesus is not our equal!), but there may be differences in maturity. For example, the apostle Paul puts himself forward as a model (1 Cor. 4:16; Phil. 3:17), but "he does not think of himself as the personal embodiment of an ideal which must be imitated."[10] In other words, Paul isn't the perfect model.

Paul does not pretend to be Jesus. He is like us, calling himself the "the worst" of sinners (1 Tim. 1:15 NIV), but he's different from us in his role as an apostle. Paul does not model spiritual perfection but models the process of having one's life shaped to be like Christ (Phil. 3:12).

God's preferred method for shaping lives is through relationships, the intentional friendships we have with others to help them to be shaped by Christ as we're shaped by Him. In other words, we invite people into the practice of following Christ, knowing that progress and not perfection is required. Walking with another is a natural way to do this. Only Jesus has the right to ask people to follow Him.

WALKING IS A WAY OF LIFE

Peggy and I waited nervously, anticipating our first parent-teacher conference. I'm not sure why we were so anxious. The teacher was a friend and enjoyed having our son Ryan in her class.

As we settled into the conversation, his teacher, Carol, said, "You know, Bill, not only does Ryan look like you, he also talks like you, and he even walks like you!" There was a way about him that marked Ryan as my son. This simple observation made this dad's day!

As Jesus followers, there should be a way about how we disciple others. These ways are habitual approaches to life and ministry, a "typical manner in which someone behaves."[11] Disciplemaking, then, becomes a way of life and not a participation in a program or the completion of a curriculum. This way of life moves disciplemaking from the "Great Option" to the Great Commission. We habitually invite people to walk with us in this life of discipleship. This book will help you get started in this way of life.

This way of walking is done in small steps—a **micro approach** to disciplemaking. Let me explain by telling a story.

When I was in graduate school, a senior professor commented, "I have seen a lot of educational fads come and go over the years.

The test of anything new is, does it affect the interaction between the teacher and the student in the classroom?" In other words, new conceptual programs have little impact until the exchange between one teacher and a student in a classroom is affected—this is change at a micro level.

This book will not address the big-picture issues of worship, programming, or discipleship curriculums. These are important topics and others have addressed them. I'm writing about "micro" ministry—what takes place when we come alongside one, two, or three people and invite them to walk with us as we walk with Jesus. We're drawing people into a small circle of relationships for a period of time to learn together how to live Jesus' life and mission. This is intentional, micro ministry done through relationships.

Over the past five decades, I've learned some things about micro ministry, simple principles to relationally disciple others. I wish I had known these lessons when I first started my disciple-making journey. I won't pretend that by following them you or your ministry will suddenly explode. No, these are insights and principles, not prescriptions for growth.

What are these ways?

We walk heart-to-heart.

We walk simple.

We walk slow.

We walk deep.

We walk on mission.

We start with **heart-to-heart**. Inviting people to walk with us always flows from our love for God and travels in the friendships of loving others. Why is simplicity important? Keeping it **simple** brings a clarity that starts small, selects wisely, and stays focused.

Experience has taught me that disciplemaking can't be programmed, scheduled, or plotted on a chart. It's a **slow** partnership with the Holy Spirit. When we invite people to walk with us, we want something more than people practicing a set of Christian disciplines or adopting a moral code. We seek a **depth** in our friends' lives—something that shapes the inner soul of a man or woman.

Finally, we can practice four of the five principles—heart-to-heart, keep it simple, slow, and build deep—but if we don't live on **mission** we've failed. Our Lord always wants to use our lives for the advancement of His kingdom where we live, work, or play.

You may be an experienced disciplemaker. If so, this book will focus your intentionality and upgrade the excellence as you invite people to walk with you in the path of discipleship. You may be a beginner at making disciples. It's my prayer that this book will give you the heart, vision, and know-how for a lifetime of making disciples.

> "Walk with me" is an invitation that intentionally draws one, two, or three people into a small circle of relationships for a period of time to learn together how to live as Jesus' disciples—experiencing His life and mission. Walking practices five simple principles— we walk heart-to-heart, simple, slow, deep, and on mission.

CHAPTER ONE

PRINCIPLE 1—
WE WALK
HEART-TO-HEART

*The Puritans spoke about a
"comfortable walking with God."*

JAMES HOUSTON

The Mowry family is a dog family. We've always had dogs in our home. Our current one is a rescue dog, a Treeing Walker Coonhound named Ginger.

Ginger was abused by her previous owner, so it's taken a couple of years for her to bond with us. She is especially fearful of men, retreating from any personal sign of affection from me. We've had to teach her the pleasure of being petted. Appreciating the gentleness of my touch was a learned reaction because a hand gesture once meant an act of violence.

Now one statement makes her literally jump for joy. "Ginger, let's go for a walk!"

Coonhounds love walks. Walks are adventures for them.

Ginger puts her nose to the ground and savors the novel scents, smells that are different from those in our backyard. Walking is a sensuous experience of new scents and sights.

Walking Ginger has been part of the bonding process between the two of us. She knows that the invitation to walk will be a pleasurable one. I've become someone to be enjoyed, someone to be trusted, someone who loves her. Walking is great exercise for both of us.

Walking is something more than what we do with a dog. Walking is a universal metaphor for relationship building, whether with other people or with our heavenly Father. Eugene Peterson writes:

> Instead of walking straight to a destination by the shortest route, it suggests a casual walking around . . . conversing with a friend . . . This is the form the verb takes in Genesis that shows God out for an evening stroll in Eden, anticipating a conversation with Adam and Eve . . . He wasn't headed for a destination. He was entering into a place and time for relaxed conversation.[1]

When we invite people to walk with us, we're inviting them into our walks with God, the heart of who we are. We walk with God heart-to-heart and we walk with people heart-to-heart.

THE "HEART" OF HEART-TO-HEART

Dan's intensity caught me off guard. I was expecting a casual conversation about his work and church ministry. Dan wanted something more. "Jeannie and I are really struggling with our son," he confided. "We deeply love him but the attention and care that his special needs require is driving a wedge between my wife and me. I return home from work to an exhausted wife, an overactive kid, and no time to myself. We're trying to trust God, but our son's needs are overwhelming us."

In the space of about twenty minutes, Dan opened his heart to me about his frustrations, anger, and lack of communication with Jeannie. His transparent pain set aside any notions about my trying to sugarcoat his pain to make me look wise. He was hurting, and he needed a friend to talk to.

OUR HEART IS THE CORE DEPOSITORY OF OUR PASSIONS, OUR INNER SECRETS, AND OUR HIDDEN DESIRES. IT IS IN OUR HEARTS THAT LIFE TAKES PLACE.

I felt honored to be invited into Dan's heart of hearts. When people open up their hearts, real ministry happens. It's at that moment that we need to connect Jesus to the issues of a person's heart. Heart-to-heart speaks to the depth of who we are. It reflects our passions and connects emotionally with others.

Heart-to-heart ministry should not be unusual. After all, it's been documented that the word "heart" is found over seven hundred times in the Bible. Engaging our hearts is so important that we're commanded first to love God "with all your heart" (Matt. 22:37 NIV) and to seek Him with all our heart (Jer. 29:13). Jesus taught that the evil that comes from people comes from the heart (Mark 7:21). That is why the Lord gives us a "new heart" to love Him (Ezek. 36:26).

Our heart is the core depository of our passions, our inner secrets, and our hidden desires. It is in our hearts that life takes place. We can disguise it with our surface actions or expressions but they simply hide the true reality of what's in our hearts.

We truly "see" one another when we peer into one another's hearts. Our hearts reveal what we love, and when we find what people love, we see the person for who he or she really is. As author Steve Garber puts it,

> It is why Augustine's long-ago question still rings true: you cannot really know someone by asking "What do you believe?" It is only when you ask, "What do you love?" that we begin to know another.[2]

An examination of our hearts tells us what we hold most dear and what motivates us for either good or evil. When we speak of heart-to-heart ministry, we engage with people at the most personal, passionate, and revealing parts of our being. Simply put, living heart-to-heart is what friends do. When we invite people to walk with us, we invite them into our hearts.

Dan felt safe in our relationship, so he invited me to peer underneath the covers of his life to see his heart. When we minister heart-to-heart with people, we engage them at a deep level of trust and openness. To build those kinds of relationships means engaging with another in heart-to-heart ways.

HEART-TO-HEART STARTS WITH GOD

"You shall love the Lord your God with all your heart
and with all your soul and with all your mind. This is the
great and first commandment."
—Matthew 22:37–38

Remember the eleven men on the hillside in Matthew 28? Remember how they obediently waited at Jesus' pre-appointed location?

When the Lord showed up and the disciples saw Him, "they worshiped him" (Matt. 28:17 NIV). We don't know what this worship looked like, but we know it was probably spontaneous and heartfelt. No one had instructed them to do this, and the Master did not require it.

What can we learn from this example? Before Jesus issued the command of "Go and make disciples," the men showed their love for Him through worship. Here's a basic principle: the Great Commandment of loving God always precedes the Great Commission of making disciples. If we don't get this priority right, we will fail to minister in heart-to-heart ways. Loving God is the bottom-line requirement for passing on the faith to others. Love is the "royal law" of the kingdom (James 2:8).

Author and pastor John Piper gives a wonderful description of what it means to love God with all our hearts:

> I define loving God mainly as treasuring God. That is, it is an experience of cherishing, delighting, admiring, and valuing. . . . Love for God is an affair of the affections . . . an affection of the heart.[3]

Jesus so values this love that He rebukes the Ephesian church because, as He told them, "you have left your first love" (Rev. 2:4 NASB). No one wants this accusation leveled against them by the Lord. How can this happen to a life? Let me describe how it happened to me.

Consider this: how many sermons do you remember? I've heard a lot of messages in my lifetime but one stands out.

I was halfheartedly listening to Lucas, a guest speaker at church, when he made a statement that caught my attention. "It's easy for us to perfect the *means* in the Christian life but miss the *end*," he said. The Holy Spirit nudged me to pay attention.

Lucas described how we can live the Christian life by erroneously focusing on perfecting the "means" to knowing God. What did this look like to me? I had developed my discipleship checklist. I was working on my prayer life, trying to read the Bible more, and looking for ways to share my faith. I was focusing on quantity (how long did I pray?) and technique (did I share my faith the "right" way?), and not on my relationship with God. Praying and witnessing are good to do and they're biblical, but I realized that I was missing the "end"—loving God. I was perfecting the Christian disciplines but not loving God! I began to seriously think about what it meant to love Jesus and not perfect the disciplines of the spiritual life.

This Holy Spirit moment shifted my heart from doing to loving.

HEART-TO-HEART IS A GODLY PLEASURE

Lucas's message showed me that I'm a recovering perfectionist. I've been working to change this condition ever since. Like anyone in recovery, I needed a new "why," a new motivation to replace my former one of mastering the Christian life. The Lord opened my heart to Psalm 27:4, using this passage to chart a path to recover my first love.

> One thing have I asked of the LORD, that will I seek after: that I may dwell in the house of the LORD all the days of my life, to gaze upon the beauty of the LORD and to inquire in his temple.

I want the psalmist's passion to be my passion—seeking God should be my number-one priority. Now, notice what the author wants to find in this search. He wants to "gaze upon the beauty of the LORD."

Things of beauty always draw us back to look or taste again and again. We have favorite songs, restaurants, or scenic spots that draw us back like iron filings to a magnet. That's what it means to me to treasure our Lord. I'm drawn back again and again to taste His goodness and beauty. This lifestyle is more soul-filling than one of mastering the spiritual disciplines.

OVER A CENTURY AGO, THE WORDS USED TO DESCRIBE OUR BREAKTHROUGH INTO A PERSONAL RELATIONSHIP WITH JESUS WERE: "I WAS SEIZED BY THE POWER OF A GREAT AFFECTION." ISN'T THAT A THRILLING STATEMENT!

The Puritan authors referred to the beauty of the Lord as *suavitas*, Latin for "sweetness." To appreciate beauty is not simply an abstract idea but a genuine feeling of pleasure, a sweetness of the heart.[4] Our hearts become emotionally engaged in the object of beauty. As Christ followers, knowing God is the sweetest thing we can experience.

What makes our Lord so attractive, so pleasurable? We use a variety of words for becoming a Christian today. We talk about "being born again," "receiving Christ," or "accepting Christ." Over a century ago, "the words used to describe the breakthrough into a personal relationship with Jesus were: 'I was seized by the power of a great affection.'"[5] Isn't that a thrilling statement? Because we've been seized by a great affection—God's love—we respond from our hearts to Him.

Disciplemaking is fundamentally about helping people love God and live for Him. What changes lives is not my ministry competencies, my assured answers, or my moral conduct. It's my life in Christ, a life "seized by a great affection," a life passed on from one person to another. Like the apostle John, we want to take the life we have in Christ and invite people into fellowship "with the Father and with his Son Jesus Christ" (1 John 1:3). This is true heart-to-heart ministry. This is what it means when we invite people to walk with us as we walk with Jesus.

Our love for God is the well from which all life and ministry flows. Jesus promised to be the one who fills this well, satisfying the thirst of our hearts so that "out of his heart will flow rivers of living water" through us (John 7:38).

I fill this well by treasuring my Lord, cherishing Him for who He is, and experiencing His sweetness. This cherishing needs constant renewing and refreshing. James K. A. Smith quotes writer Geoff Dyer who said, "your deepest desire is the one manifested by your daily life of habits."[6] This daily life of small habits can be the key to loving God.

HEART-TO-HEART NEEDS SOME LOVE HABITS

Each of us has a routine when we get up in the morning. Some of us head for our cup of coffee, others pick up the paper to check the headlines, and some (like me!) take the dog outside. Routines hold our lives together.

Author Jean Fleming writes that our lives are "held together by a web of habits that have become nearly automatic."[7] Consciously or unconsciously, we fill our lives with habits and routines, so most of them are now automatic. These small habits are necessary because, as Jan Johnson puts it, "disciplines provide personal space in which relationship is worked out."[8]

Peggy and I have celebrated forty-five years of marriage. Because I work out of our home, we see each other frequently during the day. We seem to always be present with each other. However, this alone doesn't guarantee a good marriage. We can pass each other repeatedly during the day and never have a conversation. Being present in the same place and time does not equate to loving another.

To maintain our love, we've settled on some daily and weekly disciplines. Daily, we take time to talk. Weekly, we go out for a date night. These simple disciplines keep our love focused and refreshed. It's the same way in our walk with God. We need to make regular investments into our love relationship with Him. I like to call these investments, these disciplines, our "love habits."

I have several love habits for investing in my love for Jesus. One in particular has sustained my life for five decades. Here's how it got started.

When I became a Christian in my sophomore year in college, Ed introduced me to the practice of a "quiet time," a designated time during the day to read the Bible and pray. It was easy to maintain this habit when I was around friends in our campus ministry who practiced a quiet time and kept me accountable. This changed when I returned home for summer break and my network of Christian friends evaporated.

Left on my own, my time with God soon became one of fond memories. Work, time with former friends, and the lack of accountability had put my time with God on the shelf . . . until I picked up a certain book.

Tucked under a stack of papers and vinyl records in my bedroom was a small, inexpensive book titled *The School of Obedience* by a nineteenth-century author, Andrew Murray. At the end of the book was this challenge: Can you spend the first thirty minutes of every day alone with God? Are you willing to make this sacrifice? I still have this time-weathered book, which has been reprinted and reissued countless times. The original cover price of mine was fifty cents, and my pencil underlining is still present. Here's a passage that leapt out at me:

> Christ asked great sacrifices of His disciples; He
> has perhaps asked little of you as yet. But now He
> allows, He invites, He longs for you to make some.

> Sacrifices make strong men [and women]. Sacrifices
> help wonderfully to wrench us away from earth and
> self-pleasing, and lift us heavenward.[9]

God grabbed my heart. I decided in the summer of 1970 that I would get up each morning and have my time with God. I could schedule time during the day or before I went to bed, but I wanted to make the sacrifice to seek Him in the morning, to give Him the first portion of my day.

WHAT ARE YOU DOING TO INVEST IN YOUR FIRST LOVE?

Have I been 100 percent perfect in maintaining this daily habit? No, but I bet I'm around 75–80 percent over five decades. I can't imagine what life would be like if I didn't maintain this simple love habit.

Have I lost motivation at times? Yes. Is every morning a life-changing experience? No. Can I make this a "means," a simple checkoff in my spiritual life? Of course. I have to work at keeping this time fresh in both vision and practice.

In heart-to-heart ministry, we recruit people to live the Great Commandment. Without a love for God we have a dry, mechanical faith that doesn't impart life to others. Let me ask you the same questions I ask others: What are you doing to invest in your first love? What love habits are you practicing to feed your soul and to treasure God? When we invite people to walk with us, we invite them into a heart-to-heart relationship that starts with loving God.[10]

HEART-TO-HEART
MEANS LOVING MY NEIGHBORS

"And a second is like it: You shall love
your neighbor as yourself."
—Matthew 22:39

Stan is one of the most spiritually influential people I know. He's not a popular speaker, seminar leader, or bestselling author. Stan is a small-business owner in southern Ohio. He simply loves his neighbors, living in heart-to-heart ways.

For Stan, loving his neighbors starts with his family. I've never met anyone who is so committed to ministering to his extended family as Stan is. He tells me story after story of spiritual conversations and practical service to his siblings, children, nieces, nephews, and grandchildren.

Loving his neighbors extends to his church family where he disciples men and mentors leaders. His neighbors include people at work, where he loves and cares for each employee, sharing his faith in Jesus in appropriate ways, discipling people in the workplace. He regularly invites people to walk with him as he walks with Jesus.

Stan takes the Great Commandment of loving his neighbors seriously. This love is often one person at a time, one "neighbor" after another. Now, a neighbor is not necessarily someone who physically lives next door. A neighbor is anyone that I'm "next to" in a sustained relationship. They may occupy a physical space, such as a nearby house or workplace. They may also occupy a "space" in my relational network, like a sibling, spouse, or friend from church.

You would think that loving people in heart-to-heart relationships would be a given in discipling others. Stan should not be the exception. Unfortunately, our tendency to package programs and craft formulas for growth has diminished the relational side of the Great Commission. Here's an example.

After a friend met with a spiritual leader in his church, his wife asked, "So, did he ask you about your family? your marriage? your walk with God?"

"No," was my friend's sheepish reply. "At first, he asked how I was doing but we quickly moved to a discussion about church ministry. He gave some advice on my small group and encouraged me to think bigger when it came to the size of the group."

This was not heart-to-heart; it was activity-to-activity, program-to-program. When we relate this way, we're saying something about the value of people. What they do and participate in becomes more important than who they are and what God is doing in their lives. It's easy to invite people to attend a meeting; it's harder to ask them to walk with me as I walk with Jesus.

HEART-TO-HEART TREASURES PEOPLE

The apostle Paul treasured people, loving and cherishing them as friends. He knew when to love and when to pull rank as an apostle. Most of the time he loved. Heart-to-heart words easily flow from his mouth to his new converts in Thessalonica:

> He is "a nursing mother taking care of her own children" (1 Thess. 2:7).

He is like a "father with his children," exhorting, encouraging, and charging each one (1 Thess. 2:11–12).

He calls them his "dear brothers and sisters" (1 Thess. 1:4; 2:1; 2:9 NLT).

They are his "joy" and "crown of boasting" (1 Thess. 2:19).

One commentary describes how the word "crown" means the victor's crown for an athletic contest. "The only prize in life that [Paul] really valued was to see his converts living good lives. . . . Our greatest glory lies in those whom we have set or helped on the path to Christ."[11]

Paul modeled how love, expressed in heart-to-heart relationships, is the vehicle in which discipleship travels. Real people with real stories were the recipients of his endearing comments. He loved and treasured people. What does that look like today?

Kim is a pharmacist, but her life mission is passing on her faith in Christ to other women. "I made a simple decision when I was in college," she told me. "I wanted to always be discipling a woman, passing on my faith to another." Coworkers have come to faith, friends in her neighborhood have embraced the Savior, and she's even discipling a woman in eastern Europe via Skype. Kim treasures people.

Kim and her husband, Rob, have a new group of neighbors to treasure: international students at a nearby college. Here's how she describes her heart-to-heart disciplemaking ministry: "A great way to meet international students is to have lunch with them in the school cafeteria. On off days from work, I sometimes visit the cafeteria to meet with students. One of the things we've discovered is that international students love hanging out with Americans. So, Rob and I take them apple-picking with us, or we invite them over for Thanksgiving dinner, or Rob recruits them to help him with yard work." Because they treasure people, they invite people into their lives.

Heart-to-heart ministry loves our neighbors, inviting them into our lives, walking with us as we walk with Jesus. They can be people who are exploring Christ or people in whom Christ lives. Kim and Rob are not doing this because of a church's program. They voluntarily spend their time with people because that's what Jesus' disciples do. When we love God, we will love our neighbors in heart-to-heart ways, inviting them to walk with us as we walk with Jesus.

HEART-TO-HEART IS INTENTIONAL

Loving people in heart-to-heart ways is a nice ideal, but how do we get started? We can start by practicing a little **TLC**—transparency, listening, and caring.

Transparency

Remember my friendship with Ed? One of my most vivid memories was a conversation with him that happened before I came to faith. I was studying in my dorm room one afternoon and Ed knocked on the door to come in and talk.

"I have to talk with someone," he said.

"What's up?" I replied.

"I just lied to a good friend and my conscience feels terrible," he admitted. "I have to talk with someone about this."

I'm thinking, *What's the big deal? I'm not ashamed of a little lie at times to get out of doing something.* This was my unregenerate self talking. While I dismissed the urgency that Ed felt, the conversation did get me thinking. I wasn't this honest with people about my faults. While I wasn't a practitioner of honesty, I was an admirer of Ed's transparency.

Author Philip Yancy writes, "Relationships deepen as I trust my friends with secrets."[12] A mark of a rich friendship is the ability to share our secrets, our lives together. Consider the example of Jesus.

In Luke 22:28 (NIV), Jesus takes His disciples away from the crowds and says, "You are those who have stood by me in my trials." Picture the scene. Jesus has experienced the triumphal entry to Jerusalem, He has kept the Passover meal with the Twelve, and a disciple has left to betray Him. It is in this context that He expresses His appreciation for the disciples standing by Him.

Did you notice that His comment to the Twelve is in the past tense ("who have stood")? It appears that He wasn't talking about the cross because the cross hasn't happened yet. What was He referring to? We know that He "in every respect has been tempted as we are" (Heb. 4:15). From the desert to the garden, from the road to the upper room, He constantly faced an overwhelming temptation to sin. A personal compromise would torpedo His mission. This drove Him to prayer (Heb. 5:7) and to confide in His closest companions.

What can we conclude from this? Observe what the Lord affirms with the Twelve: "You have stood by me." Standing by someone means more than standing next to them physically. We "stand by" people to support, encourage, and love them when they face trials. How will people know when to stand by us? They know because we tell them about the trial and we ask for their help. How could the Twelve know to stand with Jesus unless He was transparent enough to let them know what He was suffering?

Transparency takes place within relationships of trust and commitment. We could describe transparency as "a willingness to expose my personal struggles, fears, and life issues inside the safety of a [loving] friendship."[13] Transparency invites people to walk with me, as I walk with Jesus, in heart-to-heart and committed ways.

Here are some simple steps to initiate transparency:

What is a current joy that I can share with someone?

What is a current concern that I can share with someone?

Is there a temptation or sin that I need to confess or ask for prayer from someone?

What is a current source of discouragement or a challenge to share with someone?

Listening

The second part of TLC is listening. Several years ago, Peggy asked me to get my hearing checked during my next physical. "Sometimes I don't think you're hearing me," was her concern. Guess what? My hearing was fine but my listening was off. I heard but did not listen.

Listening is a biblical virtue. James puts it succinctly: "My dear brothers and sisters, take note of this: Everyone should be quick to listen, slow to speak . . ." (James 1:19 NIV). I have a plaque I keep on my desk to remind me of the importance of listening. It reads:

LISTEN INTENTLY. QUESTION DEEPLY. SPEAK CAUTIOUSLY.

How can we listen well? These simple actions help.

- Pause before answering. I'm too often quick to speak but not quick to hear. A momentary pause helps me focus on the question or statement before I feel compelled to reply.
- Ask another question. It's a bit of a cliché that good teachers answer questions by asking questions. I return questions with questions to help understand what a person is asking. I ask questions to clarify or illustrate what the problem or inquiry is.
- Restate what someone else asked. This is called framing or reflective listening. We reflect back to a person what he or she said so that we are clear about the question or statement. Restating or reflecting back shows we are listening.

Restating or reflecting must be done cautiously and not mechanically. My friend Grady had attended a workshop on reflective listening and was trying to practice it in everyday conversations. As he sat across from a friend at breakfast, practicing reflective listening, the friend pushed his plate back and said, "I don't know what you're doing but I wish you would stop repeating what I just said!"

We build heart-to-heart relationships when we listen well (without merely echoing back what people say!).

Caring

In practicing a little TLC, we demonstrate care in relationships. We care by choosing to be empathetic. Empathy is "the action of understanding, being aware of, being sensitive to, and vicariously experiencing the feelings, thoughts, and experience of another."[14] Putting myself in the heart and mind of another means choosing to feel with them what they're experiencing. Empathy can start with asking two basic questions: What is the other person thinking? and What is the other person feeling?

Empathy moves the focus off myself and onto another person. When I can understand how a friend thinks or feels, then I can take a practical action step and care for them.

Caring happens in small ways. Our friends Mike and Karen are struggling with some family issues. Karen unexpectedly received a phone call one day from two friends who said, "We're taking you out to lunch today!" These friends considered the stress that Karen was under—they were empathetic—and they chose an ordinary act to show they cared. The time laughing and sharing their lives over lunch (which Karen didn't have to pay for!) refreshed her in the midst of family challenges. She felt cared for. We engage people heart-to-heart when we care.

Heart-to-heart is up-close and personal. Educator and author Howard Hendricks wrote: "You can impress people at a distance. But you can impact them only up close. And the closer you are to them, the greater and more permanent the impact."[15] We get close to people through a little TLC.

TO WRAP UP: REMEMBER TLC

Living heart-to-heart is costly. It means intentionally giving up time, preferences, and energy to help another grow in Christ. For private people like me, we have to open up a little bit about our private worlds. We choose to move toward others even when they may not naturally move toward us. We choose to ask questions rather than talk about ourselves. We choose to spend time with people when we might prefer some personal down time.

I often pray Paul's "life-and-death" challenge:

> For the love of Christ controls us, because we have concluded this: that one has died for all, therefore all have died; and he died for all, that those who live might no longer live for themselves but for him who for their sake died and was raised.
> —*2 Corinthians 5:14–15*

Loving our neighbors is a life-and-death challenge. It happens in practical ways, through transparency, listening, and caring. How can you practice being a good neighbor to someone this coming week? What will it take to do it in heart-to-heart ways? How can you practice some TLC? We invite people to walk with us as we walk with Jesus, and we do it in heart-to-heart ways.

WALK HEART TO HEART

TRANSPARENCY

Share a joy
Share a concern
Share forgiveness
Share a life burden

LISTEN

Pause
Ask
Restate

CARE

Be empathetic
Love in small ways

CHAPTER TWO

PRINCIPLE 2—
WE WALK SIMPLE

Any fool can make something complicated.
It takes a genius to make it simple.

WOODY GUTHRIE,
AMERICAN FOLKSINGER

The sign on the pharmacy's counter caught my attention. It outlined all the benefits and potential hazards of a particular drug. While I appreciated the pharmacy's concern, I couldn't read the page. The text was so small that a magnifying glass was needed to read it. The minuscule print filled an entire page! I stood there thinking, *There has to be a simpler way to inform customers.*

We live in an age of complexity. Want to test this reality? Sign up for a new smartphone plan! A study in the Netherlands "found that nearly half of the products returned by consumers for refunds are in perfect working order, but their new owners couldn't figure out how to use them."[1]

Consider the workplace's supreme value of multitasking, which is, obviously, performing several tasks at the same time. It's assumed that more can be accomplished at a faster pace! Unfortunately, when we make a virtue of multitasking, our brains run in a hampered state. The reality is that our brains crave attention and focus in order to work. In other words, we think better when we think slowly.

Our cultural explosion of choices in both our personal and public lives creates anxieties and often induces decision-making paralysis. This cultural complexity extends to the church.

In visiting a pastor recently, I noticed a stack of books and video series lining the entire front of his desk. What was the subject matter? The books and videos were about how to disciple others. Jeff was searching for the holy grail of disciplemaking—the one perfect program that guaranteed results. Unfortunately, this abundance of choices created confusion. We've missed the wisdom of Leonardo da Vinci, who is quoted as saying, "Simplicity is the ultimate sophistication."

How we disciple others should run counter to our culture's obsession with complexity. We invite people to walk with us in simple ways.

SIMPLE DISCIPLEMAKING IS FOCUSED

I googled recently to find out how many words are in the Old Testament. What was the answer? One source told me that the King James Version has 783,137 words in the Old Testament. Jesus did something remarkable. He condensed the teaching of nearly 800,000 words to fourteen (twenty-three if you count the "for this sums up" phrase):

"So in everything, do to others what you would have them do to you, for this sums up the Law and the Prophets."
—*Matthew 7:12 NIV*

I asked Google another question: "How many commandments are in the Old Testament?" The Talmud (a Jewish commentary that includes the Old Testament and additional rabbinic teachings) notes that there are 613 commandments. Jesus cut to the chase when He addressed which were the greatest of these six hundred–plus commands. He synthesized them into two:

"'Love the Lord your God with all your heart and with all your soul and with all your mind.' This is the first and greatest commandment. And the second is like it: 'Love your neighbor as yourself.' All the Law and the Prophets hang on these two commandments."
—*Matthew 22:37–40 NIV*

Simplicity is the ability to get to the core, the essence of a subject. When we achieve the core of something, we discover a greater sense of clarity. We realize what is really important. Simplicity helps us focus. Alan Siegel describes simplicity in this way:

When you reach a point where you have achieved **transparency** (laying bare the underlying truth whatever it reveals), **clarity** (expressing meaning clearly and simply), and **usability** (making something fit for its purpose), you have . . . achieved simplicity.[2]

Simplicity strips out the excess stuff in order to make room for the things that are most important. It methodically distills the excess to the essential. Jesus modeled simplicity. He stripped out all the excess of the Old Testament, leaving us with two great commandments. He achieved transparency, clarity, and usability. Jesus keeps it simple so that we can focus.

Now, there's a difference between simplicity and being simplistic. When pressed, Jesus could expound on and justify how He arrived at these twenty-three words and two commandments. We see His knowledge of the Old Testament as He talked with the disciples on the Emmaus road. As they traveled, He takes them on a tour of the Old Testament (Luke 24:27). Wouldn't you have liked to have eavesdropped on that conversation? He did not repeat the fourteen words as a slogan but provided the biblical backdrop, the big picture of His life and mission.

WHEN WE HAVE CLARITY AND COMMITMENT, WE CAN COMMUNICATE MORE EFFECTIVELY.

Simplicity is something more than a slogan on a baseball cap or T-shirt; it's a reasoned and simply stated conclusion drawn from study or analysis. Being simple is about synthesis, clarity, and importance. In contrast, being simplistic means living by a bumper sticker.

The complete works of the eminent twentieth-century theologian Karl Barth log in at over forty volumes. The story is told that when asked about the main message of the Bible, Barth replied: "Jesus loves me, this I know, for the Bible tells me so."

If challenged, Barth could justify his statement by the sheer weight of his writings. His life study got to the core of the Christian message without being simplistic. Barth would echo the sentiments of Albert Einstein, who pronounced, "Nature is pleased with simplicity." The kingdom way is a simple way.

Simplicity brings clarity to complexity. Simplicity examines the complex to get at its core. It captures the essence behind all the "stuff." When we make something clear, getting at its core, we encourage commitment. Simplicity helps us prioritize the most important.

When we have clarity and commitment, we can communicate more effectively. Successful consumer brands operate on this principle. The Nike swoosh or the Macintosh apple are simple designs that instantly communicate. I've found that the greater the complexity, the less likely something will be understood and applied. We lose focus when things become complex. Simplicity keeps us focused.

So how does simplicity impact disciplemaking, asking people to walk with us as we walk with Jesus?

SIMPLE DISCIPLEMAKING STARTS SMALL

People were Jesus' strategy. "His concern was not with programs to reach the multitudes, but with men whom the multitudes would follow. . . . He literally staked His whole ministry on them [the twelve disciples]," writes Robert Coleman.[3] People were Jesus' strategy.

When surrounded, crushed, and pressed by the crowds as shown in Mark 3, Jesus took an unusual step. He could have placed Himself at the head of a movement that was personality-based and popularized by crowds (Mark 3:7, 9, 20). The momentum was there. Instead, He stepped back and invested in a few people (Mark 3:13–14). I call these people "kingdom extenders."

Jesus would extend His rule and reign not by bigger crowds but through individuals He had discipled. This decision was a turning point in His ministry. Our Lord stepped back from the crowds to relationally invest in twelve men, intentionally focusing on a few. What a simple strategy!

This simple strategy had a small beginning, but it was worldwide in scope. Jesus commissioned these men to go to "all the nations." The universal church is a tribute to these men fulfilling that mission . . . and it's still happening today.

Brian calls himself a "small" person living a simple but focused life. Being small has nothing to do with his height but his lifestyle.

Brian started living this simple life when he was in college. "I decided that my ministry was the guys on my dormitory floor," he told me. "I made it a point to build friends and share my faith with these few men. I'm still in touch with most of them today. Thinking small helped me invest my time and energies into a few. Instead of seeing how many people I could know, I kept it simple by thinking small." Brian invited a few men to walk with him as he walked with Jesus. He kept it simple by staying small and focused.

As Brian moved into adulthood, focusing on his family was another way to live simply. "I made it a priority to love and disciple my children. As a grandfather today, I'm still thinking small and investing in my children. It keeps my goal in life pretty simple." Brian's personal ministry to his family is now multiplying. He helps other fathers think small, helping them disciple their children.

Living simple and focused extended to Brian's vocation. "I

decided to master a few things in my career, **SIMPLICITY IS**
choosing to be a model of excellence in a **A LIFE FOCUSED**
few things. This kept my career simple by **AROUND A FEW**
thinking small." **IMPORTANT**
Simplicity for Brian meant living small **THINGS.**
and focused. He didn't layer his life with
ever-increasing commitments and activities. Brian practiced
what author Greg McKeown calls "essentialism." Essentialism
is the disciplined pursuit of less. Essentialism believes that "by
investing in fewer things we have the satisfying experience of
making significant progress in the things that matter most."[4]

Brian kept life's priorities simple: befriend a few, invest in your
family, master your work, pass on your life to others. Simplicity is
a life focused around a few important things.

I call this "small-circle disciplemaking." Jesus intentionally drew
twelve men into a small circle. Within this circle, He shared His
struggles (Luke 22:28), invited them into His private moments of
glory (Luke 9:28–29), and explained His teaching outside of the
crowd's peering eyes (Mark 4:10–12).

Our churches and ministries are casting about for strategies
based on bigger budgets, more buildings, and the hiring of ministry professionals. Jesus demonstrated the power of relationships,
investing in a small circle of people who would then multiply their
lives into the lives of others. The simplicity of His strategy is still
relevant today.

The way of simplicity starts with a small circle of people.
Small-circle disciplemaking invites one, two, or three people into
a discipleship group, asking them to walk with us as we walk with
Jesus. We relationally and intentionally invest in these men or

women, focusing on the few rather than the many. What is our goal? Our goal is pretty simple and is explained in a picture.

SIMPLE DISCIPLEMAKING
HAS A CLEAR PICTURE

Let's play the word association game. When I say the word "disciple," what image comes to mind? For many Christ followers, this word is not part of their conscious goals. In a nationwide survey by the Barna Research Group, the researchers asked people to describe their goals in life. Almost nine out of ten described themselves as Christians. "But not one of the adults we interviewed said that their goal in life was to be a committed follower of Jesus Christ or to make disciples."[5] Could it be that we have not communicated a simple picture of a disciple?

Pictures are powerful communicators. As has been stated, "The human mind is not, as philosophers would have you think, a debating hall, but a picture gallery."[6] Good communicators use images and pictures to tell their message. Jesus was a master at doing this. He described His kingdom through pictures—a sower, a woman searching for a lost coin, a mustard seed. A picture is worth a thousand words!

"Images are a powerful and natural way for humans to communicate. . . . We are hardwired for understanding images and using images to communicate . . . There seems to be something inside of us—even from an early age—that yearns to draw or otherwise show the ideas in our head through imagery," asserts author and communicator Garr Reynolds.[7]

Those fourteen words of Jesus are pretty straightforward. At his or her core, a disciple loves God and loves their neighbor. Pretty simple, isn't it? How could we picture this command? An illustration I consistently use is The Navigators Wheel.[8]

The Navigators Wheel™

A wheel communicates no matter where we go or who we're with. Let me give you a tour of this wheel. The hub of the wheel is what provides the power and movement forward. For the disciple, loving Jesus is the center of one's life (Gal. 2:20). I'm always seeking to invest in my first love.

What practical steps help us love God? Loving God happens when we practice the two vertical spokes of prayer and the Word (the Bible). After all, Jesus modeled prayer throughout His life (Mark 1:35) and expected His words to "abide" in His followers (John 15:7). These are the "means" for us to love God.

Now for the second commandment. The horizontal spokes represent our relationship to our neighbors. One spoke is witnessing, engaging people in faith conversations about Jesus (1 Peter 3:15). The other spoke is the love we have for other believers expressed in biblical fellowship (John 13:34–35; Heb.10:24–25).

One spoke extends to those for whom Christ died. The other spoke goes to those in whom Christ lives. Obedience is the rim that ties all of this together. Obedience is the action that demonstrates our love for the Savior (John 14:21).

I love the wheel because it keeps the picture of a disciple simple—Jesus followers love God and love their neighbors. This illustration also gives flexibility in presentation and in content. I can take a napkin or a piece of paper and draw out the wheel to anyone at any time.

The wheel can also be a tool for self-evaluation. A simple way to assess where someone is as a disciple is to ask her to draw out the wheel, lengthening a spoke to illustrate a strength or shortening a spoke to picture an area of growth. This lopsided wheel tells both of us the condition of their discipleship.

This simple strategy for passing on our faith starts with a relationship within a small circle of a few relational investments. Our aim is helping people love God and love their neighbors. A wheel pictures the goal of disciplemaking: a direction to take people on our walk that is not haphazard or whimsical but focused. Now for the question lingering in everyone's minds: Who do I invite into this disciplemaking circle?

SIMPLE DISCIPLEMAKING
STARTS WITH SELECTION

Two women showed up at Peggy's invitation to join a Bible-reading group. Both were eager to get started. Both wanted to read the

Bible. Both lamented how life had pushed reading the Bible to the back burner of their schedules.

They got off to a great start. Sue and Christy were taking the time to read the Bible. They talked about encouraging their children to read the Bible. They were making time for this simple discipline. But Sue's interest began to wane.

"I can't make it today because of work demands." "I can't come today because I didn't have time to read the assignment." "I can't come today because my boss called a lunch meeting." Sue found one reason after another not to meet with Peggy and Christy. Some were legitimate but many could have been worked around. Sue soon dropped out, but Christy remained.

Christy showed up. Sure, her work periodically interfered with the lunch meetings but the majority of the time she showed up. Peggy and I have learned to invite people who "show up" into our small circles of disciplemaking. This is one of my takeaways from the Great Commission passage in Matthew 28:16 (NIV). "Then the eleven disciples *went to Galilee, to the mountain* where Jesus had told them to go." They showed up!

THE "QUALIFICATIONS" FOR WHO TO INVITE INTO OUR SMALL CIRCLE OF DISCIPLEMAKING IS PRETTY SIMPLE. WE LOOK FOR PEOPLE WHO SHOW UP AND FOR PEOPLE WHO ARE EAGER TO LEARN.

Look for people who faithfully show up.

Besides showing up, Christy was eager to learn. She was usually prepared. She asked questions about the text. She acted on her discoveries.

When we talk about disciplemaking, we're talking about people who are "learners." The Greek word *discipulus* means one who learns, who follows, who is ready to open up to the new.[9] Disciples want to learn about Jesus, they want to learn from Jesus, and they want to learn to follow Jesus. Disciples are people eager to learn.

My friend Diane lamented the mistake she made about the women she invited into her small circle. "I chose people who I thought *needed* to grow, not those who *wanted* to grow." Sometimes those who *need* to grow as disciples may not *want* to grow as disciples. We must look for those in whom the Holy Spirit is at work, and this is often demonstrated by people who are eager to learn.

The "qualifications" for who to invite into our small circle of disciplemaking are pretty simple. We look for people who show up and for people who are eager to learn.

Now comes the commitment question: "Do I ask for a commitment from someone to walk with me?" The answer is both yes and no. If I'm inviting people into a circle of disciplemaking, a small group that meets for the purpose of shaping our lives to follow Christ, then I ask for a commitment. I expect people to come prepared (there are always assignments and work in discipleship circles), to come to participate, and to come to apply.

Sometimes I invite people to a circle of two—me and one other person. Do I ask for a similar commitment that I expect from a small group? Sometimes I ask for a commitment but generally I simply do it. I identify people in my network of relationships who show up to grow and have a hunger for life change. I invite them out for coffee or a meal. In the course of the conversation, I inquire about their walk with God, their progress in maturity, and how they're living on mission. I then issue a simple invitation. "How would you like to regularly meet to talk about what it means to be Jesus' disciple today?"

If they say yes, I set up our next meeting. I may or may not use a curriculum, as I would with a small group, when I walk with someone one-by-one. However, I do have a *picture* in mind (the wheel) and I do have a *process* to go deep (which I will discuss in chapter 4).

TO WRAP UP: KEEP IT SIMPLE

Inviting people to walk with us in this life of discipleship does not have to be complex. We can keep it simple. Simplicity brings clarity and commitment, and it creates effective communication. When we invite people to walk with us, we keep it small (a disciplemaking circle), we keep it focused with a clear picture of a disciple, and we keep the qualification of who to invite pretty simple: we look for people who show up and for people who want to learn.

As you consider your disciplemaking walk, keep it simple by asking these questions:

> Are you willing to start small with a few?
> Do you have a clear picture of a disciple, the destination of your walk?
> Are you wise in your selection—looking for people who show up and who want to learn?

Your rich journey in disciplemaking will be greatly enhanced as you focus on simplicity!

WALK SIMPLE

KEEP IT FOCUSED

Find the essentials
Aim for clarity

START SMALL

Invest in a few (small-circle disciplemaking)

BE CLEAR

Have a picture of a New Testament disciple

SELECT WISELY

Who shows up?
Who wants to learn?

CHAPTER THREE

PRINCIPLE 3—
WE WALK SLOW

*To be a Christian is not a matter of a moment;
it takes time.*

DIETRICH BONHOEFFER

Walking slow is an acquired value and habit for life. We want to hurry; God wants to go slow. Life is learning to live with a slow God. Walking with a God who takes His time was a difficult lesson for Peggy and me to learn.

In our first years as Navigator staff, Peggy and I knew little about fundraising. The Navigators is a "faith" mission, meaning we trust God for our income through the generous gifts of others. Since we lacked fundraising expertise, we also lacked funds. There's a correlation between the two! The first few staff years were financial challenges. We had to learn to walk with a slow God.

LEARNING TO WALK WITH A SLOW GOD

Walking with a slow God touches all of life—even finances. In our first years on staff, Peggy felt the financial pinch the most. She had to feed us from our meager income. Baked beans, pancakes, and other low-income meals were our staples.

Like a good campus missionary, I kept plugging away in ministry, meeting with students on campus while Peggy tried to balance the checkbook. On one particular day, I met with Clay, a college freshman. Sitting in a dormitory study lounge to read the Bible, we chose Deuteronomy 8 to read. There was no particular reason for the choice of this passage. After reading the text, these verses jumped off the page to me:

> "And you shall remember the whole way that the LORD your God has led you these forty years in the wilderness, that he might humble you, testing you to know what was in your heart. . . . And he humbled you and let you hunger and fed you with manna . . . that he might make you know that man does not live by bread alone, but man lives by every word that comes from the mouth of the LORD."
>
> —*Deuteronomy 8:2–3*

I was jolted out of my chair when I read those statements. God seemed to be speaking to me directly: "Bill, I'm letting you and Peggy go hungry to teach you a lesson. It's more important to learn how to live by My Word than to have a full stomach." Like He did with Israel, God was letting us go hungry to teach us a character lesson, but it was going to take a while. For Israel, it was forty years! Now I had a fresh perspective on our life situation. I didn't go home for a steak dinner, but I had some meaning for our financial trials.

The Lord called Israel to remember how He had led them . . . for forty years! This was not an overnight, snap-of the-fingers life change, but forty years of watching the cloud by day and the fire by night. This was a slow walk over four decades. He humbled Israel, letting them hunger but always providing food in timely ways. What was the lesson? He wanted Israel to learn to trust Him by taking Him at His word. The Lord wasn't in a hurry to teach this lesson. This wasn't a neatly defined ten-week Sunday school course.

Peggy's and my financial need did not clear up overnight. We learned day by day to take the Lord at His word. Years later we're still learning this lesson. Spiritual change doesn't happen overnight, and there is no injection for quick life change. Little by little, we're slowly learning what it means to trust God. I sometimes wish God could zap us with changed character but that's not His usual way. We need to learn to walk with a slow God.

When we invite others to walk with us in the Jesus life, we're entering into a slow journey. Disciplemaking is not for those who want quick results, a programmed curriculum, or guaranteed success. Disciplemaking is sometimes two steps forward and one step back. We must learn to walk slowly with God and with others.

Ministering in slow ways means that we slow down to see people as individuals. When we do this, we learn to love people according to how God has designed them and the pace of growth He has for their lives. Disciplemaking means learning how to walk with a slow God, but our culture has another speed.

WE LIVE FAST

Unlike kingdom culture, speed is the nature of our American culture. We want faster internet, faster smartphones, and faster purchasing power. Overnight and sometimes same-day delivery are becoming the norm for most businesses. This zeal for speed is having implications far beyond our obsession for faster internet service and consumer purchases—speed is impacting our ability to adjust and adapt to life.

In his book *Thank You for Being Late*, author Thomas Friedman describes how in the past we had time to adapt to scientific and technological progress. Incremental steps allowed us to keep up with the changes around us. However, things have now changed.

> [Edward Teller, who designed the hydrogen bomb, surmised], "A thousand years ago, it probably would have taken two or three generations to adapt to something new." By 1900, the time it took to adapt got down to one generation. . . . Today, said Teller, the accelerating speed of scientific and technological innovations can outpace the capacity of the average human being and our societal structures to adapt and absorb them. . . . Change is now accelerating so fast that it has risen above the average rate at which most people can absorb all these changes. Many of us cannot keep pace anymore.[1]

The pace of change is all around us. We see it in sexual mores, economic changes, media, and a fundamental reshaping of such institutions as work, marriage, and even church. Historian Noga Arikha laments this loss of security due to speed: "The world I took for granted as a child, and that my childhood books beautifully represented, jerks with the brand new world of artificial glare . . . [everything is now] faster, louder, unrelated to nature, self-contained."[2]

Many of us feel lost in this new world of speed. We sense that a life of hurry is a life of superficiality. We discover that "hurry always empties a soul."[3]

Our culture is becoming one science fiction writer's reality. A book that's probably read by most high school students is Ray Bradbury's *Fahrenheit 451*. In Bradbury's imagined future, books and the homes of book owners are burned by firemen. Only a brave few keep the act of reading alive by hiding books, hoping to escape the firemen.

Why were books hated and feared? When a fireman quizzed a book owner on this question, he answered that it was because of leisure. "Oh, but we've plenty of off hours," was the fireman's reply. "Off hours, yes. But time to think? If you're not driving a hundred miles an hour, at a clip where you can't think of anything else but the danger, then you're playing some game or sitting in some room where you can't argue with the four-wall televisor. . . . [The televisor] is immediate, it has dimension. It tells you what to think and blasts it in. . . . It rushes you on so quickly to its own conclusions your mind hasn't time to protest."[4]

Doesn't this sound like a page from today? We get our thrills from extreme sports, we vicariously live through celebrities or reality TV, and we love our video games. Our minds do not have time to protest. We need some leisure!

Leisure forces us to slow down to reflect and think. The Chinese character for "leisure" is made up of "space" and "sunshine." It denotes the pause, the attitude of relaxation that creates a gap in life so the sun can shine through.[5] In contrast, the Chinese ideogram "busy" is made up of two characters, "heart" and "killing."[6]

In foretelling our multitasking, media-drenched, and thrill-seeking world, Bradbury believed that fighting the life of speed meant slowing down, opening up space in our lives to think. If we don't, busyness will kill our hearts, and speed will harm how we walk with and disciple others. We must learn to walk slow.

WE HAVE A SLOW GOD

God does not seem to be in a hurry. Consider Israel's conquest of the promised land. They had been waiting hundreds of years for God to fulfill the promise He gave to Abraham in Genesis 12:1–3. Could God's timing have been any slower?

Centuries after the promise, as we read in the book of Exodus, we find Israel on the verge of entering the land God had promised to them. Anticipation was building. Was God going to snap His fingers and give Israel the land? Here's His strategy (Ex. 23:29–30):

> "I will not drive them out [the Hivites, Canaanites, and the Hittites] from before you in one year, lest the land become desolate and the wild beasts multiply against you. Little by little I will drive them out from before you, until you have increased and possess the land."

Do you notice that our Lord had a different strategy than a quick conquest? Israel was not ready to acquire the land. Instant success would be their downfall. If God were to wave His hand and drive out the land's inhabitants, nothing would be left. The small and fledgling nation of Israel would face a barren land, an expanse soon to be overrun by wild beasts and weeds. Our Lord had another plan, one that made more sense to a small nation. "Little by little," the practice of slowness, was God's strategy.

Here's the kicker to this verse. Not only would it be little by little, but it would take decades. Soon after this promise in Exodus, Israel would rebel against God and He would delay the acquisition of the promised land by forty years (Num. 14:20–24). He wanted Israel to learn the lesson of trust and that building trust takes time. It goes slow.

Now fast-forward to Deuteronomy 7. Israel is ready to go into the land. The Lord again promises that He "will clear away these nations before you little by little" (Deut. 7:22). The promise was about to be realized, forty years later.

Nation development is not the Lord's only application of slowness. Becoming more like Christ—spiritual maturity—is a little-by-little approach. Pastor and author Eugene Peterson writes: "Maturity cannot be hurried, programmed, or tinkered with. There are no steroids available for growing up in Christ more quickly. Impatient shortcuts land us in the dead ends of immaturity."[7]

Another analogy is the seepage of water into a crevice. Author and poet Esther de Waal suggests that "the journey into God was a matter of seepage, slow seepage, an advancing tide, not some sudden event with a climatic point."[8] Character development is a slow, patient process. We walk with a slow God.

Our Lord is capable of speed. In an instant, He can heal, rescue, or provide. However, there is ample biblical and experiential evidence to suggest that slow is God's preferred speed.

We must learn to keep pace with a slow God. Sometimes His timing is not our timing. My timing usually reflects my desire for immediate gratification. His slowness is a commitment to people's welfare, patiently waiting for them to love Him. Our compulsive timetables sometimes collide with God's patient providence. Slowness is a virtue to our heavenly Father and a countercultural value to life today. We walk with a slow God.

WE PRACTICE SLOW

Slowness means adapting to the spiritual pace of people. Patience is slowness applied. We can only move as fast as the Holy Spirit works in someone's life. My friendship with Dean was no exception.

We had known each other for years. Dean knew that I was a Christian. Even though we shared life together with our children, sports, and our wives' friendship, there was never an apparent interest in spiritual things on his part. Then the sports banquet came up on my schedule.

A local ministry was sponsoring an event where a popular football coach would talk about his faith. I prayerfully decided to invite Dean.

After the meeting was over, Dean turned to me and said, "Thanks for inviting me. Work has been crazy. I needed to hear this message." I was surprised at his quick response. I issued another invitation: "I'm inviting a group of men to read the Bible with me. Would you be interested?" "I'm ready for something like this," was his prompt answer.

This conversation was probably twenty years in the making. Slowness means coming alongside the interest and the pace of people. Four easily remembered steps have helped me practice slow. I remember things better when I create acronyms for memory cues. Here's an acronym for living slow.

> **S**erve excellently
> **L**ove accordingly
> **O**bserve to learn
> **W**ait for God's timing

Serve Excellently

You've read about my perfectionistic tendencies. Peggy reminds me that I need to stop analyzing and enjoy the tasks that I accomplish. Because I have a compulsion to make things better, I'm often unsatisfied and critical of what I've done. I'm learning to pursue the virtue of excellence rather than perfection. Perfection can never be attained, but I can do things excellently . . . but excellence requires slowness.

TO DO THINGS WELL WE MUST SLOW DOWN AND RETURN TO HIGH QUALITY BASICS.

Excellence implies doing something extremely well. Excellent work has a sense of beauty and elegance to it. Excellence speaks to my doing the best I can with the resources and abilities available. While excellence does not require perfection, it does require work and effort.

Paul exhorts us to "strive to excel in building up the church" (1 Cor. 14:12). In Colossians 3:17, we're exhorted to "do everything in the name of the Lord Jesus." The thought here is that acting in the name of a person means acting as that person's representative. The name of Christ makes the smallest task something noble and honorable, something beautiful and fresh.[9]

When we invite people to walk with us as we walk with Jesus, we act as Jesus' representatives, serving in His name. We should model the one who left people "astonished" because He did "all things well" (Mark 7:37).

To do things well we must slow down and return to high quality basics. The wise author Oswald Chambers describes our task this way: "We have to be exceptional in ordinary things, to be holy in mean streets . . . and this is not learned in five minutes."[10]

A model for being exceptional is found in the legendary Shaker furniture. Shaker furniture is marked by its simplicity, a lack of ostentatiousness, and quality workmanship. Their philosophy is pretty straightforward:

> Make every product better than it's ever been done before. Make the parts you cannot see as well as the parts you can see. Use only the best of materials, even for the most everyday items. Give the same attention to the smallest detail as you do the largest. Design every item you make to last forever.[11]

Isn't this a great description for disciplemaking? Walking with others means engaging in the "parts you cannot see." These "parts" are the unseen conversations and acts of love hidden from the public's attention. These small acts should have the same attention to detail as a rousing worship service.

Everyday ministry should demand the best materials and deserves our full attention. After all, when we invite people to walk with us, we are Jesus' representatives, and He did everything well. Excellence requires the virtue of slowness.

Serving with excellence marked the life of my father. Dad came to faith in his early forties. When he surrendered to Christ, he only knew one way to live life—the way of commitment and excellence. He was a craftsman, trained as a meat cutter (or butcher) in a Louisiana packinghouse during the Great Depression of the 1930s. He naturally transferred the skills and commitment to excellence from his job to his new faith.

For thirty years, Dad taught Sunday school, led small groups, and spoke around the state of Ohio as a representative of the Gideons, the organization known for placing Bibles in hotel rooms. My parents had high school educations and no formal training in ministry. They were the "little" people of chapter 2, everyday people in the normal routines of life, inviting others to walk with them as they walked with Jesus.

When my father passed away, he did not leave a large inheritance. I received his Bible study books, commentaries, and a file of his small group Bible study lessons. As I thumbed through these materials, I found the books marked up, passages underlined, and teaching notes filled with discussion questions.

A great deal of thought and preparation had gone into his everyday ministry of leading a Bible study in his mobile home community and teaching Sunday school in a small country church. My mind wandered back to seeing him retreat to his study after work and spend hours studying his Bible and preparing the lessons. He put time and effort into his ministry—a ministry hidden away in an ordinary place, a ministry done slow and with excellence.

How can we walk slow with excellence? Here are two steps to consider.

1. Have I intentionally prayed? This is not a "Lord, bless this time" but a concerted approach to pray through every main point, every Scripture used, or every question asked.

2. Do I know the material? While you may not have professional training in the Scriptures, ask yourself if you've put the due diligence into your preparation so that you know the material well.

Love Accordingly

People are different. This is obvious, but sometimes we fail to practice its reality. It's more efficient to treat everyone the same, expecting that people share the same faith trajectory, and need the same Bible content or spiritual experience. When we practice slowness, we take into account people's individual differences and love them accordingly.

Both of my sons are trained illustrators. As a teenager, our older son, Jason, always felt a little out of place in the traditional classroom until a high school art teacher introduced him to right brain/left brain thinking.

This philosophy of education teaches that the two hemispheres of our brain are wired in different ways. The left side is our analytic, linear, sequential side. The right side of the brain is our intuitive, picture making, synthesizing side.[12] Most of our educational settings are designed for left-brain thinkers. We put people in rows, teach sequentially, expect logical answers, and give little time for daydreaming or experimentation. Can you begin to sense how right-brain people might struggle?

"Now I understand why I always felt a little out of place in the classroom," was Jason's discovery when realizing he was a right-brain thinker. This realization freed him from the guilt and constraints of traditional learning to explore art in new and fresh ways—ways that reflected how he learned.

When we disciple others, inviting them to walk with us as we walk with Jesus, we must understand that one size does not fit all. Everyone grows differently, is motivated differently, and matures at different speeds. Ministering in slow ways means that we slow down to see people as individuals. When we do this, we learn to love people according to how God has designed them and not treat them as projects.

Paul understood this simple principle of loving accordingly. He described it in this way:

> And we urge you, brothers and sisters, warn those who
> are idle and disruptive, encourage the disheartened,
> help the weak, be patient with everyone.
> —*1 Thessalonians 5:14 NIV*

How do we love the idle? We warn them of the consequences of idleness. How do we love the disheartened? We provide words of encouragement. How do we love the weak? We help them in practical ways. Bottom line, we're to be patient with everyone since patience is Paul's first mark of true love: "Love is patient . . . " (1 Cor. 13:4) Patience loves people according to their needs and spiritual maturity. Patience is slowness applied.

Several years ago we sponsored an alumni picnic for former students in our campus ministry. At the end of the day, I thought, *Jesus, You could return now and I would leave a blessed man!*

It was so satisfying to see men and women I had known when they were eighteen, nineteen, or twenty years old, now mature, some married with children. The maturity I had longed for in their lives was in full bloom.

My mind went back to their time on campus where I pushed, pulled, and cajoled them to get with the program and grow! I leaned on them to make the next commitment, the next step of faith. I lacked patience. I was unwilling to let some of them grow at the rate God had for their lives. Slowness is a tension between desiring the next step for people and waiting for God's timing for those steps.

Slowness is applied when I treat people as individuals. I take time to get below the surface when growth seems delayed. Take the example of Jake. Jake was a regular attender in my Bible study. However, I noticed he seldom completed his study assignments. In fact, he rarely read the Bible. "Reading the Bible is just not something I enjoy," he said.

In a casual conversation one day, he revealed that he had a learning disability and had spent a lifetime learning to cope with it. Knowing a little about learning disabilities, I asked him how it was demonstrated in his life.

"I struggle with tracking words from left to right when I read.

Words tend to jumble up on the page and I have to really focus to move from word to word and not get lost."

"Can I see your Bible?" I asked. It was a standard study Bible laid out with three columns on each page. Two columns were the biblical text, and the center column was for cross references. When you opened the Bible, six columns showed up across two pages. For someone with dyslexia, this layout would make your head spin.

"Is reading this difficult for you?" I asked.

"You bet it is," replied Jake.

I purchased a Bible for him that had only one column per page. Now he could read the Bible with greater ease and pleasure. What he considered a spiritual problem—"I don't like reading the Bible!"—was really a learning issue. Because people are different, we take the time to treat them as individuals, fitting into the story that God is working out in their lives. Walking slow means loving and discipling people according to who they are.

How can we love accordingly? Here are two simple approaches.

1. Learn people's faith stories. Ask people to draw out a timeline listing the people and events that have shaped their lives. This simple exercise will help you discover the unique story behind each person.

2. Spend time individually with people. If possible, visit someone at work. Seek to understand what their day is like. Visit them at their home or apartment. You will understand a lot about someone from observing how they live, decorate, and prioritize their spending on possessions.

Observe and Learn

One of my long-distance mentors is the novelist, poet, and agrarian philosopher Wendell Berry. Berry writes that slowness and paying attention is at the heart of the successful farmer . . . and person.

Successful farming starts with a simple act: walk the land. Farmers don't run, they walk. Slow walking allows the farmer to pay attention so that he or she can truly care for the farm.

"The gait most congenial to agrarian thought and sensibility is walking. It is the gait best suited to paying attention . . . and most permissive of stopping to look or think. Machines, companies, and politicians run!" wrote Berry with a little tongue in cheek.[13] *Solvitur ambulando* goes the Latin tag: "You can sort it out by walking."[14]

Slowness is a virtue to the farmer. He or she knows that as speed increases, care declines. "The faster we go the less we see. This law applies with equal force to work; the faster we work the less attention we can pay to its details, and the less skill we can apply to it," Wendell Berry states.[15] Again, as speed increases, care declines. Slowness is necessary for successful farming.

The farmer's leisurely gait in order to observe and pay attention is our model for inviting others to walk with us as we walk with Jesus. A farmer doesn't look only to enjoy the scenery but to study the land in order to care. By caring, the farm will flourish. In the same way, we want to look at others, slowing down to care, looking to nourish a life.

I've often pondered the statement by Jesus that "you will indeed see but never perceive" (Matt. 13:14). How can you see without perceiving? For Israel, they saw a man from Nazareth and missed the Messiah. They observed but didn't really look. I've discovered that I often see but seldom look.

I've found two ways of seeing. One way is simply observing what is there. My wife, Peggy, has brown eyes, she's wearing a blue sweater, and is carrying a bag of groceries. She's stopping to chat with a neighbor. My sight scans this neighbor and records the observable details: she's wearing jeans and a hooded sweatshirt, she's holding her dog's leash, and she's looking serious. I've noticed her outward appearance, but I don't know what's happening in her life. Seeing into a life is what I call "soul sight."

Seeing with the soul notices what's happening in a person's face and posture. Their eyes tell me whether they're happy or sad. The turn of a mouth tells me their mood. Body language reveals their true feelings. Soul sight is the type of observation that we practice in discipling others. Soul sight happens when we slow down to practice heart-to-heart relationships.

"You seem a little down today, Brad." I had noticed that Brad lacked his usual enthusiasm. He didn't greet me with his customary smile and strong handshake.

"I'm discouraged. There are so many demands on my time that it's hard for me to get to sleep at night. Besides work and the kids, I signed on to coach a middle-school soccer team. I also have duties at church, and my dad is needing my help for a rehab project at his house. I really need to sort out my priorities."

"Want to talk about it some more?" I asked. When he said yes, I took us to Mark 1:29–39. We made some observations about Jesus' priorities in a twenty-four time period where He was pushed and pulled by the expectations of others. We noted how

Jesus made prayer a priority (v. 35) and He had a clear sense of His mission (v. 38). "What can we learn from His example that can apply to our busy lives?" I asked.

A simple observation turned into a discipling moment. We talked about the lordship of Christ and the importance of prayer—all spokes of the discipleship wheel. A discipling movement started by my exercising soul sight.

Looking is a small act of dying to self. I'm choosing to give my attention entirely to another person and not worry about my own agenda. I want to look so that I can understand and love the other person, not advance my own goals or interests. In looking, I can respond with a sympathetic presence, encourage with an appropriate word, or exhort if appropriate. This all starts by observing with soul sight. When I truly learn to see, I can begin to connect Jesus to a life.

How can we slow down to observe and learn?

1. Watch a person's face. What animates them? Is the mouth turned up or down? Is their gaze focused or blank? What do you notice about the current state of their soul?

2. Ask an appropriate question. Questions could include: "I notice you're a little discouraged. What's going on?" "You look happy today. What's causing the joy?" "You seem a little puzzled. What's the issue?" We can ask appropriate questions because we have first looked.

Wait for God's Timing

It's breakfast on Tuesday and time to meet Craig at our favorite coffee spot. He wants to grow in his faith but sometimes lacks motivation. He knows that the Bible should be important, but he doesn't have the discipline to read it. God has become more of a life concept than a relationship. How can you love a concept? I was praying and waiting for the "right" moment to challenge him. This moment came when the roof caved in on Craig's life.

The collapse happened in the rhythm of work. As a new manager, Craig was stretched. There were new expectations and greater accountability. Craig found himself tethered to his smartphone, working 24/7. Anxiety was building. He couldn't sleep, he stopped paying attention to his children, and he lost weight. The Lord had Craig's attention. Because I was walking with him in a relationship, I spotted an open door for ministry and walked in.

Timing is everything. Did you know that the New Testament uses two different words to express the Hebrew concept of time? *Chronos* time is chronological time. It refers to quantity of time or the amount of time passed (Matt. 25:19). *Kairos* time is about the "right" moment (Mark 1:15) or the moment of opportunity. Kairos time speaks "of those opportune times that become turning points."[16] A kairos moment had happened in Craig's life.

Kairos thinking is when we realize that our days and hours are full of moments for advancing God's kingdom if only we have wisdom enough to see the possibilities and seize them accordingly. Teachers call them "teachable moments."

These possibilities are often connected with the natural

rhythms of life. Instead of points on a timeline, the Bible depicts time as a series of constant rhythms:

> Seedtime and harvest,
> cold and heat,
> summer and winter.
> —*Genesis 8:22 NIV*

> For everything there is a season, and a time for every
>   matter under heaven:
> a time to be born, and a time to die;
> a time to plant, and a time to pluck up what is planted.
> —*Ecclesiastes 3:1–2*

Life is wrapped up in these rhythms. There's a time for sowing and reaping, there's a time for cold and heat, there's a time to plant and a time to pluck. Timing is everything. We have a rhythm in our careers, our marriages, and our relationships. When we invite people to walk with us, we enter into a friend's life rhythms and wait for the kairos moments. This happened with my friend Craig.

Because I had stayed in relationship with Craig, walking with him through life, I seized the kairos time. To deal with stress, I encouraged him to read the Psalms. What was once academic now became a heartfelt reality. Out of desperation, he fled to God's refuge.

My experience with Craig reinforced two lessons for walking with people. One, I had to wait to catch the kairos moment with him—that teachable moment inspired by the Holy Spirit. We spent several Tuesdays together before this moment arrived.

Second, I seized the moment because I was walking with him. We spot kairos moments when we're heart-to-heart with people, paying attention to what God is doing, walking alongside them as we go through life. It's difficult to spot a kairos moment from behind a pulpit or lectern. It usually happens when we're up close and personal, walking next to people. Kairos moments can be seized now but sometimes they require our waiting in faith. We must remember that our efforts are never wasted but the results may be delayed . . . for decades.

Nate's dad had his son's life mapped out. He sent Nate to a private college, expecting academic and professional success. Then God intervened. Nate became a believer in his sophomore year. Having his son become what he called a "fundamentalist Christian" was not part of his father's plan. Neither was Nate's next move. He decided that God was calling him to the pastorate.

Nate's decision shattered his father's dreams and strained their relationship. For over thirty years, Nate couldn't talk with his father about his faith. They had a cordial but cautious relationship. Then the kairos moment happened.

Nate's father became seriously ill in his early eighties. Nate's stepmother contacted him for help. Together, they mapped out a plan of action with the physicians to deal with his father's declining health. In the process of caregiving, Nate's dad began to open up about his life. This was the kairos moment. Nate stepped into this rhythm of the Spirit and initiated several faith conversations with his father.

This story has a happy ending. Nate's dad came to faith. As life's fourth quarter wound down for his father, Nate took the initiative one last time and had a gospel conversation with his dad. We go slow, patiently trusting God that our efforts are not wasted but sometimes delayed.

How do we wait for God's timing?

1. Be on the lookout for kairos moments. We can think that growth only happens in "spiritual places"—a church service, a Sunday school class, or in a small group. God creates teachable moments on the job, in the daily commute, with our friends or spouse, or through our hobbies.
2. Be patient. This may be a time of sowing in someone's life. Your effort is not wasted, the outcome is just delayed. Remember, the fourth quarter still needs to be played.

TO WRAP UP—WALK S.L.O.W.

We serve a slow God. When our culture pushes the hurry-up disciplemaking button, forcing you to conform to the world of speed, respond with this shout of "Walk S.L.O.W."!

I will

Serve with excellence!

Love accordingly!

Observe and learn!

Wait for God's timing!

WALK SLOW

SERVE EXCELLENTLY

Pray comprehensively
Know the material

LOVE ACCORDINGLY

Know another's faith story
Spend time with people

OBSERVE AND LEARN

Soul sight
Soul questions

WAIT FOR GOD'S TIMING

Look for *kairos* moments
Practice patience

CHAPTER FOUR

PRINCIPLE 4—
WE WALK DEEP

*Superficiality is the curse of our age. . . . The desperate
need today is not for a greater number of intelligent
people, or gifted people, but for deep people.*

RICHARD FOSTER

W e waited for the phone call with a mixture of anticipation and anxiety. Our son's call would announce the birth of our grandchildren—twin boys! But anxiety hung over the wait. Our daughter-in-law had been warned that she could give birth quite early. We would be proud grandparents, but the boys might be dangerously premature. How should we anticipate the call?

The twins were born at twenty-six weeks, weighing one and a half pounds apiece. They were so small they couldn't be held for any length of time outside the incubator. They spent seven months in the hospital's prenatal care unit. Our son and daughter-in-law spent hours in the hospital, watching the monitors, observing the boys' blood pressures, heartrates, and breathing.

The challenges didn't end when the boys came home. Our son

and daughter-in-law lived with the anxiety that each baby might require more specialized surgery. Worry dominated each of our lives. Peggy and I had to dig deep because we were in uncharted waters. Our beliefs and convictions were tested.

My mind was flooded with questions: "Why did our children have to go through this?" "Why couldn't our grandchildren have a normal life like other babies?" "When could we enjoy our grandchildren like other grandparents enjoyed theirs?" How did we make it? The Lord preserved us through our daily routines.

Peggy and I had three practices that gave us hope throughout this experience. One was counting on friends who supported and prayed for our children and grandchildren. Another was having books we read that fed our souls. Finally, we continued to practice the daily routine of coming into God's presence, giving Him time to speak to us through His word and prayer. In all these, the Lord showed up and encouraged us.

You've probably experienced what the prophet spoke of in Isaiah 30:21: "And your ears shall hear a word behind you, saying . . ." The Holy Spirit has a word for us in our darkest moments. He had one for me.

In one of my discouraging days, the Holy Spirit highlighted this verse in my reading time: "Rejoice in hope, be patient in tribulation, be constant in prayer" (Rom. 12:12). I realized at that moment that I needed to pause and rejoice in the hope of the boys' future growth. I needed to be patient in this tribulation (to live slowly) and I needed to keep praying.

But wait, the story of Romans 12:12 isn't finished yet. In a very unusual way, God cemented this passage in my life.

As a diversion from our anxiety, Peggy and I visited a local craft show. I'm usually not a fan of craft shows—the endless booths of photographers, landscape artists, and linoleum painters don't do much for me. Out of boredom, I paused at a woodcutter's booth. She had engraved quotes on repurposed pieces of wood. Guess what quote caught my eye.

On a piece of barn siding was engraved Romans 12:12. Who could have orchestrated this! I paid the $30 and took the sign home. It now hangs over the doorway in my study so that whenever I look up from my chair I see Romans 12:12, encouraging me to hope, to be patient, and to keep praying.

The routines of life are our support in tough times. These routines flow from our convictions, those things we deeply believe, value, and practice. When we invite people to walk with us as we walk with Jesus, we ask them to "live out of the depths rather than the shallows."[1] A deep life is a life of conviction.

A SAD STORY OF FAILED CONVICTIONS

We all have favorite verses in the Bible, verses that give hope, cheer, or encouragement. But there are some sad verses. Here's one of the saddest passages in the Bible for me.

> And the people served the LORD all the days of Joshua, and all the days of the elders who outlived Joshua, who had seen all the great work that the LORD had done for Israel. And Joshua . . . [was] buried within the boundaries of his inheritance in Timnath-heres. . . . And there

arose another generation after them who did not know the LORD or the work that he had done for Israel. And the people of Israel did what was evil in the sight of the LORD and served the Baals. And they abandoned the LORD.

—Judges 2:7–12

Life was good for Israel as long as Joshua and the original elders were alive. But then something happened. Another generation grew up abandoning the Lord for the worship of Baal. How did this happen?

I think the generation after the elders watched from afar but lacked the conviction of their leaders. This generation did not have a front-row seat to God's miracles. While the memories of the exodus lingered in their cultural rituals, they never "owned" the faith of their elders. Like many in our culture today, they lived "off other people's spirituality rather than taking the time to develop their own direct experience of God."[2] They lacked personal conviction about a loving loyalty to God. They lived from the shallows and not the depths.

A CONVICTION TAKES WHAT'S VALUABLE AND MOVES IT INTO DAILY PRACTICE.

Convictions represent the core beliefs and practices that keep us from being people who are "double-minded" (James 1:8). This is the person of two minds, one whose allegiance is not committed either way; both sides look good. There is a lack of "moral and spiritual commitment, the devotion of our whole loyalty to the Lord."[3]

In its simplest definition, a conviction is something we're convinced of. We believe it so deeply that it becomes a daily practice of a priority. Convictions put personal values to action. Values describe what's really important to us, but they need to go a step further. A conviction takes what's valuable and moves it into daily practice. Convictions are those bedrock beliefs and practices for which we live or die. Convictions mark the life of deep people, people who are followers of Jesus.

When we invite people to walk with us as we walk with Jesus, we invite them into a life of convictions. Deep people live from firmly held beliefs and values—beliefs and values forged in a walk with God that's tested in everyday life. How do we practically grow convictions in our lives and in the lives of others?

IT STARTED AT THE DENTIST'S OFFICE

Theresa, my dental hygienist, had one message at each appointment. "Bill, you need to floss more." Who hasn't heard this exhortation? We've all heard about the importance of flossing, but a lot of us don't take it to heart. I believed in flossing but didn't practice flossing.

What turned a belief into a conviction of practice? For me, it was an extreme diagnosis. "Bill, if you don't deal with this gum disease now, your gums are going to recede and you will lose some teeth." Now she had my attention.

I had to take some steps to turn my belief about flossing into a practice of flossing. The Lord used flossing to teach me how to grow a conviction. I learned that convictions grow through engaging our hearts, heads, hands, helps, and building habits. Who would have guessed that a visit to my dentist would become a case study for conviction-building?

Step One: Inspire the Heart

Convictions are built when God inspires a heart.

I have two strong motivators, two strong desires: I want to avoid pain, and I want to look good. When Theresa showed me pictures of what my mouth would look like if gum disease continued, I was inspired to change. My motivation about pain and appearance kicked in. My heart was engaged.

As we saw in chapter 1, the heart is really important. Author James K. A. Smith writes:

> What if, instead of starting from the assumption that human beings are thinking things, we started from the conviction that human beings are first and foremost *lovers*? What if you are defined not by what you know but by what you *desire*?[4]

The center of gravity of the human person is located not in the intellect but in the heart. As Smith writes, "The heart is the existential chamber of our *love*, and it is our loves that orient us toward some ultimate end."[5] What we love, what is at the center of our hearts, is what propels our lives. Isn't this what Jesus taught, "For where your treasure is, there your heart will be also" (Matt. 6:21)?

Our heart becomes an engine driving us forward and a homing beacon pointing the way to what is most important. The need for flossing had to start in my heart. Building Christ-centered convictions must start with the heart, in my life and in the lives of others.

Inspiring a heart has one boundary: I cannot change someone else's heart. No matter how hard I try, how competent I am, or how motivational I can be, I can't change a person's heart. This is the work of the Holy Spirit. But I can catch their heart's attention. I can provide fuel to fan the heart's flames. How does this happen?

We all need inspiration. The root meaning of "inspire" in the Latin means to "in-flame" or "blow into."[6] Because my heart can grow cold, hard, or complacent, I need a constant infusion of inspiration, the Holy Spirit "in-flaming" my heart. As I discussed in chapter 1, I must be drawn back again and again to savor that which is beautiful and loving.

I have a simple practice to keep my heart inflamed. I read heart-filled books about loving God. Every day in my time with God, I spend five or ten minutes reading an inspirational book. (I've listed some of my favorites in the appendix.) I'm not interested in learning more *about* God from these books (that's another kind of reading), but I want to feed my desire *to love* God. I want my heart to be lifted from the doldrums of my routines, my preoccupation with the anxious present, or my failures of obedience to hear again how the Father loves me, forgives me, and sends me out to the world with a renewed heart.

When I invite people to walk with me as I walk with Jesus, I want to inspire them; I want to throw some logs on the fire of their hearts for the Holy Spirit to blow on and ignite. This ignition happens in different ways with different people.

My career with The Navigators has always involved the training or mentoring of leaders. I have discovered that one size does not fit all when it comes to inspiration. Seth was a leader who loved responsibility. The bigger the task, the more he was motivated. Mateo was a reader. Assign him a stack of books, recommend e-books, share relevant blogs to study, and he was ready to go. Darrell thrived with social interaction. Invite him over for lunch or to play some basketball, and you had his heart.

Now, inspiring a person's heart can become a manipulative project. Our own motives must be unmasked as we invite people to walk with us as we walk with Jesus. Touching the heart can be a tricky business. Paul gave some simple guidelines in 1 Thessalonians 2:1–6 on how *not* to motivate people:

- Don't motivate from "error." We don't twist truth to influence behavior in a certain direction.
- Don't motivate from sensuality ("impurity"). We don't use flirtation or casual intimacy to influence behavior.
- Don't motivate through false promises or unrealistic expectations ("to deceive"), trying to trick people to change behavior.
- Don't motivate because of what we can gain—popularity, finances, prestige.
- Don't motivate by pretending to be someone we're not in order to influence toward a certain goal.

Bottom line, our motivation is to be like the purity of a mother nursing an infant or a father charging his children (1 Thess. 2:7, 11). We inspire and motivate people to follow Jesus in tender, compassionate, and truthful ways.

As we invite people to walk with us as we walk with Jesus, we must understand what logs to throw on the heart's fire for the Holy Spirit to ignite. Each person is inspired in different ways. Here are some simple questions to identify the fire-starters for a life.

Is he or she motivated by reading or hearing? What inspirational books, blog posts, or podcasts can I provide?

Is he or she motivated by the urgency of the task? How can I create an urgency of ownership?

Is he or she motivated by close friendships? How can I get close enough to inspire and refresh?

Is he or she motivated by the examples of others? What stories can I tell or people can they meet for inspiration?

Is he or she motivated by words? What words capture their attention and grab their hearts?

When we invite people to walk with us as we walk with Jesus, we invite them into a deep life. This deep life is one of convictions, those rock-bottom beliefs and practices that make us people of God. Convictions start when God inspires a heart.

Step Two: Inform the Head

Convictions are built when I thoughtfully engage with the Bible.

My strongly held desires for pain avoidance and looking good were not enough to start me flossing. I knew that my desire to do the right thing would fade as soon as I walked out the door. I needed some facts. My hygienist reviewed with me the latest research on flossing's impact on overall health. Theresa helped separate fact from fiction with research-based knowledge.

What we believe is important to building convictions. The "what" is really about the "why." We need some basic information—Bible knowledge—to sustain what's happening in our hearts, our motivation.

Our Christian culture loves "teaching." We have a celebrity list of great teachers with bestselling books. The reality is that "teaching" is often a code word for more information. With social media, we can now listen to messages, attend seminars, and work through Bible studies 24/7. Peggy has friends who attend two or three Bible studies a week! Remember the shelves sagging with books on disciplemaking? We're swimming in a sea of information.

I think the Bible looks at information in two ways: information-owned and information-applied. We will discuss information-applied in an upcoming step. For now, let's focus on information-owned. Let's watch some basketball.

I was sitting on the bleachers watching my son play in a school basketball game when Jerry, a young acquaintance, slid through the aisle and sat next to me. As we watched the game, we eased into a personal conversation.

Soon Jerry was talking about his walk with God and how the Bible was shaping his future career. It was hard pulling my attention from my son's game, but what Jerry was talking about was pretty personal.

I knew this young man's parents and their family situation, and I knew that Jerry had come through a tough spot in life. But now he was "owning" his faith; it was no longer the faith of his parents but his faith. It was information-owned.

When we invite people to walk with us as we walk with Jesus, there should always be an open Bible between us. We build convictions by filling our heads with the Scriptures . . . but there's more. Our aim is more than an accumulation of biblical facts; we aim for a life transformed by owning these truths. How do we help people own what they learn from the Scriptures?

I love the adage *telling is not teaching and listening is not learning.* Owning information means more than listening to a message. Owning information is more than giving an exhortation and a prayer. Ownership starts with some questions.

Jesus was the master question-asker. The Gospels are full of His questions. Why did He ask so many questions when He knew the answers? After all, if anyone already had the right answer, the incarnate God did.

Our Lord often knew what was in people's hearts (John 2:24–25; 5:42). Unlike us, He didn't ask questions to gain information. Therefore, His questions were not for Him but for the one being asked.

What did He want to accomplish in the listeners' lives when He asked a question? When Jesus asked questions, He was training his followers "to understand that life with the Holy One was interactive."[7] If He wasn't seeking information for Himself, then we must conclude that He was asking questions to engage us in thinking. He used questions so we would actively enter this interactive process, using our minds as well as our hearts.

Jesus followed the example of the Father in the garden in Genesis 3. The first recorded conversation between the Maker and His children were questions:

> "Where are you?" (v. 9)
> "Who told you that you were naked?" (v. 11)
> "What is this that you have done?" (v. 13)

The omniscient God knew the answers. He was asking questions to force Adam and Eve to stop, think, and own their actions.

Jesus followed this example, asking His disciples questions such as "Why are you afraid, O you of little faith?" (Matt. 8:26) or "Who is my mother, and who are my brothers?" (Matt. 12:48). These questions drew the disciples, and us, into the thinking and discovery process. Questions prodded the disciples to discover their fears and ponder who belongs to God's family. Questions help people own information because they encourage self-discovery.

When we invite friends to walk with us as we walk with Jesus, we don't invite them to listen to a set of mini-sermons; we invite them to a mutual life of discovery in the Scriptures. The invitation to walk with me is a walk marked by asking questions, helping people connect the Bible to life.

Questions vary by type and by topic. Here's an example. I want to help someone own the importance of the Scriptures in their lives—to have a conviction about the authority of the Bible. Together we might explore a passage like Psalm 119:1–15, making observations on the passage together. I will ask a variety of questions.

Heart: What can we observe about the author's heart for the Scriptures?

Analysis: What happens to a life that embraces the Law of God? What happens to a life that rejects the Law of God?

Comparison: How does this passage compare with 2 Timothy 3:16–17?

Possibilities: What could happen in our lives if we embraced the Scriptures like the author does?

Application: What would our life look like if we applied this passage in the next twenty-four hours?

I was talking with some friends after an adult class at church when Monica came up. "You know," she said, "I wish Christian instruction was less about telling me what to think and more about how to think."

I knew Monica, and I knew she wasn't denying the importance of sound doctrine. She wanted something more than another lecture from behind another podium with another set of hand-outs. Monica wanted to be challenged to think so that she could own the information. Building convictions means engaging the head—challenging people to know, think about, and apply the Scriptures. We do this by asking questions.

Step Three: Give a Hand

Convictions are built when I provide practical helps.

My hygienist was more than a motivator and a researcher. Theresa showed me how to floss properly. To further encourage the habit, she gave me some complimentary dental floss. I left the office with skills and supplies—some "hands"—for flossing. In fact, she had me floss in the chair so she could observe my practice.

She didn't know it but my hygienist practiced a basic principle of disciplemaking. When Jesus chose twelve men to disciple, He invited them to "be with him" (Mark 3:13–14). This was an invitation to live life together in order for Him to demonstrate kingdom living. Author Robert Coleman describes the with-Him principle like this: "It is well enough to tell people what we mean, but it is infinitely better to show them how to do it. People are looking for a demonstration, not an explanation."[8]

When we invite people to walk with us in this life of discipleship, we do not exhort to action without coming alongside to help and to show them how. Practical help moves us from information-owned to information-applied.

God invites us to partner with Him in the transformation process. We're exhorted to train ourselves in godliness (see 1 Tim. 4:7), we're to work out our salvation (see Phil. 2:12), and we're to "make every effort" (2 Peter 1:5) to add to our faith. One way to picture our responsibility in this process is what Dallas Willard calls the **VIM** principle.[9]

The **V** in VIM corresponds to the **vision** we need for growth. We have a desired future that we want God to do in our lives. The **I** speaks to **intentionality**; I choose to take steps for growth. Willard writes that "personal transformation rarely if ever succeeds by accident, drift, or imposition."[10] It needs intentionality. Finally, **M** is for **means**. We choose practical steps and secure appropriate resources to put into practice what we envision and what we intend.

WHEN WE ASK PEOPLE TO WALK WITH US AS WE WALK WITH JESUS, WE COME ALONGSIDE THEM TO PROVIDE SOME PRACTICAL MEANS FOR GROWTH.

My dental hygienist gave me a vision. There was a full-color picture hanging on the office wall showing a healthy mouth. I looked at this picture and decided, "I want my teeth to look like that!"

Expressing a desire was not enough. I had to choose whether to take the necessary steps to achieve that goal. Intentionality is important, but I needed some instruction, some means, on how to properly floss my teeth. Vision, intentionality, and means all came together for life change.

When we ask people to walk with us as we walk with Jesus, we come alongside them to provide some practical means for growth. This is so important that Dallas Willard writes, "Our most serious failure today is the inability to provide effective practical guidance as to how to live the life of Jesus."[11]

What can this look like in practice? When Jane invited Amanda to walk with her as she walked with Jesus, she began to probe about Amanda's life with God.

"I know I need to spend time with God. I learned about this in Bible college, but I don't practice this habit," Amanda told her.

Jane asked her how she thought the habit could be helpful.

Amanda paused a moment, then replied, "I know a time with God is important, but it's gotten to be mechanical, so I've given up."

"Do you always give up when something important becomes hard?" Jane asked.

Amanda admitted, "Well no, I don't."

"When you practiced a daily time with God, how did your life benefit?" Jane asked.

"Now that you ask it that way, I saw several benefits," said Amanda.

After some conversation about Amanda's personal experiences in the past, Jane issued an invitation. "Let's look at some passages about the benefits of spending time with God."

Walking with someone means having an open Bible between us. Jane and Amanda explored passages like Mark 1:35, 2 Corinthians 4:16, and Exodus 33:11. They talked about what characterized a walk with God and what it meant to be a friend of God. (Check out www.coachthebible.com to discover how to bring the Bible to life issues.)

The conversation didn't end after one discussion or an exhortation and a prayer. Jane scheduled a time with Amanda when they would read the Bible and pray together. Then she asked Amanda to read portions of a book on the importance of meeting with God.

As Amanda gained traction and success, Jane encouraged her to begin writing down the thoughts that God was teaching her in this time. Throughout all of this, she focused on the relationship with God (the "end") and not just the practice of reading the Bible and praying (the "means").

They spent nearly two months talking about going deep with God. Jane was building a conviction by starting with the heart, providing biblical information to appeal to the head, and then giving some hands ("means") to move Amanda forward. She was helping Amanda experience both information-owned and information-applied. This was not through a series of mini-sermons or an invitation to a seminar but it was done one-to-one, heart-to-heart.

Did you notice all the "hands" that Jane used with Amanda?

She asked questions.

She provided some biblical instruction and examples.

They prayed and read the Bible together.

She used some other resources—inviting Amanda to read a book.

She encouraged journaling.

She practiced loving accountability.

Jane gave to Amanda what Dallas Willard said was lacking— "practical guidance"—to live the life of Jesus. Do you see the simplicity of this approach? You start with a friendship, a Bible, some questions, time, a few simple resources, a memo book for a journal, and the follow-through of accountability. This is how the "hands" work in building conviction. When we build conviction, we build deep people for God.

Step Four: Provide Some Helps

Convictions are built through accountability and affirmation. Theresa had another "help" in her toolbox to make flossing habitual. She scheduled the next appointment! In two months, we would see if I had made any progress. Accountability was an additional help in building a habit.

Being a competitive person, I took the next appointment as a challenge. Since I'm also a bit of a people-pleaser, I didn't want my performance to let her down. I was determined to floss and make the next appointment successful.

Accountability through a scheduled appointment helped me build a habit of flossing. Accountability through trusting relationships is a critical help in building convictions. When we ask people to walk with us as we walk with Jesus, we invite them into a life of accountability. We help each other make choices to be faithful and provide feedback on our progress.

What comes into your mind when I use the word "accountability"? The word may bring a wave of guilt or shame into your life. We picture someone with a checklist, noting when we have succeeded or failed. We don't like to experience failure or have our failures exposed. Accountability can do both.

The reality is that we face accountability in every aspect of life. We're accountable to pay taxes, make the mortgage or rent, or do certain tasks at our jobs. There's an expectation that some things need to be done.

I think we have two misconceptions about accountability in the church. One is that our grace-orientation has been wrongly applied. Since grace is not about earning, we assume that grace does not require responsibility. We miss the truth of such passages as Titus 2:11–12: "For the grace of God has appeared . . . training us to renounce ungodliness and worldly passions." While grace instructs, I choose to renounce and move away from ungodliness.

WE ASK OTHERS TO VOLUNTARILY WALK WITH US WHILE WE WALK WITH JESUS. WE WALK BY INFLUENCE AND NOT BY COERCION.

The second misconception of accountability is applying the "or else" factor. Whether it's taxes, house payment, or job performance, someone has the "or else" factor—do this "or else!" You will be fined, you'll lose your home, or you will be fired. While the body of Christ and its leaders have an "or else" factor in church discipline, this card is played very judiciously and graciously.

You and I don't have an "or else" factor in expecting behavior from people. We ask others to voluntarily walk with us while we walk with Jesus. We walk by influence and not by coercion. We invite people to partner together in faithfulness—the true goal of accountability. Accountability is simply a vehicle for encouraging one another to be faithful to our Lord. It's not a checklist for performance but a partnership in faithfulness, a friendship with shared love and trust.

Unfortunately, even with this perspective, we can distort accountability. Here's how accountability can go astray.

We subtly use guilt, saying, "Oh, you didn't do this? I thought it was important to you."

We can manipulate by asking, "I really think this is important. Don't you?"

We withdraw our acceptance. This means silently backing out of people's lives when they don't perform, in order to shame and secure a certain behavior.

To my embarrassment, I've practiced all of these abusive actions. It's easy for a relationship to devolve into performance.

How can accountability work out in real life? How do you move from performance to relationship? Here's a conversation I had with Dennis.

For several months Dennis and I had been meeting to talk about the Bible and life. While sipping coffee at a fast food restaurant, Dennis made this statement, and no kidding—it really did happen this way! "Bill, I've been thinking about memorizing Scripture. My kids do it in Sunday school, and I think it would be helpful for me."

"Why do you think memorizing the Bible could be helpful?" I asked. (Notice the kairos moment.)

He explained, "If I could recall and reflect on certain verses at critical times during the day, I think my stress levels at work would go down."

"If you want to do this, I have an incredible tool to help," I suggested. "It teaches you how to memorize and has a simple system for remembering the verses. Let me send you a copy and you can decide if it would be helpful." (Do you see how I'm suggesting a "means" to turn his interest into reality?)

The next time we met, we walked through how to use this Scripture memory tool (using the with-Him principle). We then memorized a verse together. I asked Dennis for a realistic memory goal. "I think I could do two verses a week," he said. If you notice,

I asked him to set the goal; I didn't set it myself. This encourages information-owned. Now comes my accountability invitation.

I added that I'd stopped the habit of Scripture memory and said, "Let's meet together and talk about the verses we're memorizing. That would really help me. What do you think?"

"That would be helpful to me too," Dennis replied.

What happened the next time we met? I didn't press him with "Did you memorize your verses?" That's a performance-based question. Instead, I asked him, "How did the Lord use those verses in your life?" That's a relationship-based question—focusing on his walk with God and not the action of Scripture memory.

How did I find out if Dennis memorized two verses a week? He volunteered this during the course of the conversation. How did I end the conversation? I wanted to continue with memorization, so I asked him, "What challenges did you face in memorizing these verses? What can help you be successful this coming week?" Through questions I wanted to help him discover the practices to success. I also wanted him to know that it was a two-way street, that he was helping me too.

My vision is that Dennis's life is transformed as he submits to the authority of God's Word. He is choosing to be intentional in one practical means, Scripture memory. Now, there's one more tool or "help" for conviction building.

When I returned for my follow-up appointment, the hygienist took one look at my mouth and said, "You've made amazing progress! You've turned around your condition." I was thrilled. I walked out the door feeling good about my teeth. A little affirmation becomes a big help and goes a long way in building a habit.

Jesus practiced affirmation. When He reviewed the seven churches in Revelation, He begins by affirming five of the seven churches. He doesn't issue a recorded soundbite but makes each one personal. "I know your _____" and fills in the blank. He models affirmation that is both personal and specific.

Affirmation can also be an expression of a blessing: "In Latin, to bless is *benedicere*, which means 'speaking (*dictio*) well (*bene*)' or saying good things of someone."[12] Affirmation is speaking well of the work God is doing in another's life. This is not about self-congratulation but a humble recognition of God's work.

Notice how our Lord affirms the "character" of each church in Revelation 2. He praises a quality of life, not how they performed. These included:

> toil and patient endurance (v. 2)
>
> tribulation and poverty (v. 9)
>
> holding fast to Jesus' name and not denying the faith (v. 13)
>
> works, love, and faith (v. 19)
>
> holding little power yet keeping His word (Rev. 3:8)

Our Lord was specific, personal, and character-affirming. Affirmation goes a long way in building conviction. We affirm not because it wins the approval of people (what Jesus warned against), but we're validating how a person's character and actions are God-honoring. Affirmation conveys respect because people are so important that we watch to affirm. And besides, sometimes it just feels good when someone notices and values what we do.

When we invite people to walk with us as we walk with Jesus, we provide some helps to build convictions. These helps include accountability and affirmation.

Step Five: Build Some Habits

Convictions are habitual grooves.

Do you know the word *groovy*? In the 1960s, it was a slang word meaning *excellent, fun,* or *great*. The term is actually derived from the jazz subculture and originally referred to the smoothness of the needle going through the grooves of a record. When the musicians are together, they're in the groove. My jazz guitarist friend Jack tells me that musicians enter a groove when playing—their performance seems spontaneous and effortless.

Athletes are also "groovy" people. My friend Steven played baseball at a high-caliber, college level. He loved the feeling of settling into a pitching groove—throwing a fastball or curveball in a seemingly straightforward, habitual manner. Any of us who practices a certain skill can be in the groove. We are groovy people because we have grooves in our lives.

Now behind the groove of throwing a baseball or playing a guitar is countless hours of repetition and practice. The goal is to routinely throw the ball or play an instrument in a habitual way that it becomes second nature. Practice builds a certain quality of performance into our lives, a quality developed behind the scenes, away from the crowds, often done alone.

Grooves are found in nature. A groove is a channel cut into rock by water slowly dripping over time. The water naturally follows the direction of the groove. Repetition over time cuts a channel for something lasting. This is what we do when we build conviction in people's lives; we intentionally build channels for what lasts. These grooves or spiritual habits become the "what" of disciplemaking, the essential goals in discipling others.

Jesus hints at these grooves when He gives instructions on how to pray, fast, and give (Matt. 6:5–8, 16–18). By instructing us on how to practice these acts, He assumes that we will regularly do them. We can add to these spiritual habits the importance of meditating and studying the Bible (2 Tim. 2:15) and doing good to others (Gal. 6:9–10). These disciplines are displayed in The Navigators Wheel in chapter 3. I like to call them the **basics** of the Christian life. Every disciple should be practicing these basics.

When we invite people to walk with us as we walk with Jesus, we're inviting them into a relationship where we build some grooves, i.e., habitually practicing the basics, so people can encounter God. Author Ruth Haley Barton writes, "What I can do is create the conditions in which spiritual transformation can take place, by developing and maintaining a rhythm of spiritual practices that keep me open and available to God."[13]

Now these grooves do not earn more of God's favor, they do not make us more righteous, nor do they turn us into "super spiritual" Christians. They do not reverse God's saving grace but are simple exercises in self-discipline. As Dallas Willard writes, "Grace is opposed to earning, not to effort."[14] Discipline is making the effort to develop little routines—grooves—that channel us to God's presence and transformation.

What I call a "basic" others call a "spiritual discipline." The author Richard Foster writes, "God has ordained the Disciplines of the spiritual life as the means by which we place ourselves where he can bless us."[15]

In the midst of busy lives, we carve out space for God through prayer, Bible meditation, fasting, service, and so on. Carving out space enables us to meet God and experience the transforming effect of His Spirit. This is the motive behind what Jane did with Amanda and what I did with Dennis.

When our faith was tested by our grandchildren's health, the Holy Spirit used the grooves we had built over years to sustain us: the habits of making friends, meditating on the Scriptures, and trusting God through prayer. The grooves did not make us any more righteous, but they were channels to experience God's presence.

When we ask people to walk with us as we walk with Jesus, we intentionally help them build the convictions necessary for maturity. This is not a casual, haphazard, or I'll-wait-for-it-to-come-up-in-the-conversation event. We proactively serve as "groove" builders, building channels of habits through the practice of the basics to help people encounter God. This is the ministry of building convictions. This is what marks deep people.

TO WRAP UP: THE DEEP LIFE

The chicken or the egg?

There was a sudden cold snap in Canada. My minister friend John lives in Ottawa and, besides pastoring, has a small organic farm. On this farm he raises chickens and sells their eggs. When the cold snap happened, his egg sales dried up because it was too cold for the chickens to lay.

To encourage egg-laying habits when the temperature dropped, John added more insulation to his chicken coop and increased the heating. "I wanted to enhance the conditions for egg laying," he told me. But he added this caveat: "I can enhance the conditions, but it doesn't guarantee more eggs." He could enhance the probability of an egg harvest but not guarantee its success.

When we invite people to walk with us as we walk with Jesus, we invite them to a deep life. We intentionally enhance the conditions for depth, trusting the Holy Spirit to change lives. Like John and his chickens, wise disciplemakers increase the opportunity for depth through certain principles, but they cannot guarantee that a depth of life will happen.

Building convictions happens as we partner with the Holy Spirit and:

> trust God to inspire the **heart**
>
> provide the **head** with biblical information
>
> encourage application through the **hands** of practical tools
>
> provide the **helps** of accountability and affirmation
>
> create long-term **habits** as groove builders.

One last lesson from Theresa: she was building flossing habits for the immediate and the long-term. In the immediate, my teeth would be healthy. Long term, I would have lasting teeth. This is the life of depth. We build both for the immediate and for the long term. We model the practice of Paul: "According to the grace of God given to me, like a skilled master builder I laid a foundation" (1 Cor. 3:10). His desire was to build a foundation that would stand the test of life and the test of judgment (vv. 13–15). Building depth in people's lives helps them stand in the trials of today's life and prepares us for our standing before the Lord. We walk with people inviting them to a life of depth.

WALK DEEP

INSPIRE THE HEART

Motivate biblically (don't manipulate)
Motivate personally

INFORM THE HEAD

Information-owned not information-known
Ask questions

GIVE A HAND

Practice
V: vision
I: intentional
M: means

PROVIDE SOME HELP

Practice accountability
Give affirmation

BUILD SOME HABITS

Build some grooves
Make some habits

CHAPTER FIVE

PRINCIPLE 5—

WE WALK ON MISSION

*Back when we did these big crusades in football stadi-
ums and arenas, the Holy Spirit was really moving. . . .
But today, I sense something different is happening.
I see evidence that the Holy Spirit is working in a new
way. He's moving through people where they work and
through one-on-one relationships to accomplish great
things. They are demonstrating God's love to those
around them, not just with words but in deed.*

BILLY GRAHAM

I t started with a Bible on a desk.

I was new to the faith. I lived in a college dormitory. I saw
my friend Ed talk with others about Jesus, and I wanted to do the
same. How could I get started? I put my Bible on my dorm room
desk and waited to see what would happen.

It was a simple way to identify with Christ. The only thing
on the flat plane of my desk was a big black book labeled Holy
Bible. I prayed that people would be curious and ask me about
it. The strategy worked. The guys on the floor saw the Bible and

questioned or debated me about it. I had launched my life of mission for God.

Living on mission was easy for me as a college student and later as a campus missionary with The Navigators. You can do almost anything for the gospel with college students. I've done beach evangelism, city park evangelism, student union evangelism, and door-to-door dormitory evangelism. For entertainment on Friday nights, I took students I was discipling in The Navigators and we would walk through the dorms looking for people to talk to about Jesus. Talking with strangers and doing outrageous acts seemed to be the norm for evangelism in college.

Then I left the campus world and entered the world of my peers. I soon discovered that adults in my neighborhood were different from curious, young adult undergrads.

My boldness and zeal collapsed as I mixed with post-college adults. What seemed to work on campus did not connect with my peers who had little interest in spiritual things. The passage from Proverbs 27:14 seemed to capture my evangelistic efforts: "Whoever blesses his neighbor with a loud voice, rising early in the morning, will be counted as cursing."

I can have the greatest message in the world (a blessing), but if shared at inappropriate times ("early in the morning") and in inappropriate ways ("a loud voice"), then it won't be listened to. In fact, it can be taken as a curse. I had to reconsider my approach to living on mission and what it meant for doing evangelism. The problem isn't the message but the manner in which the message is communicated.

I was "evangelistically" challenged in the world of adults. I never considered myself as gifted in evangelism, but the campus gave me a structure to operate in. When I left the campus, I was adrift in an adult world that left me underprepared and slightly fearful.

I could not treat adults in the working world as though they were twenty-year-old college students. Did you know that the average age of someone experiencing a religious conversion is 15.6? Moreover, "for every year the non-Christian grows older than 25, the odds increase exponentially against his or her ever becoming a Christian."[1]

We typically use this data to justify the imperative of reaching children and teens. Traditional wisdom tells us that if we don't "win them" while they're young, we never will. This reality should both sadden and motivate us.

But this study reveals another side of evangelism. We're trying to evangelize adults with the same approach and assumptions that we use to evangelize children and teens, and it's not working.

For over twenty years, I've been relearning my assumptions about evangelism and what it means to live on mission as an adult and to adults. Even the word "mission" has new meaning for me. When we invite people to walk with us as we walk with Jesus, we invite them to join Jesus' mission. Disciples are marked as people on a mission.

MISSION IS NOT AN OPTION

It was like a scene from a Stephen King movie. Twelve men huddled together on a dark beach. A few torches shed light onto a horrific scene. Running toward them was a howling, bleeding, naked man. "What do you want with me?" the man screamed at the leader.

Jesus confronted a demon-possessed man (Mark 5:1–20). He and the disciples had just crossed over the lake at night and were immediately met by a "nude dude in a rude mood!" I picture Jesus intently and passionately confronting this demon-enslaved man as His disciples crouched behind Him.

We know the outcome. The demons were cast out. The man appears before Jesus "dressed and in his right mind" (Mark 5:15 NIV). This nameless figure has one natural response: "Can I follow You, Jesus? Let me go with You!" He wants to be with the one who gave him freedom and a new life. But Jesus has other plans. For no apparent reason, Jesus denies his request and sends the man on mission:

> "Go home to your own people and tell them how
> much the Lord has done for you, and how he has had
> mercy on you."
> —*Mark 5:19 NIV*

Jesus doesn't send him to another country as a missionary. He doesn't send him to preach on a street corner. He gives a simple assignment: "Tell your own people how the Lord has had mercy on you." He sent him back to his own neighborhood, his own circle of family and friends. His mission—to start faith conversations about God's mercy. This is a wonderful picture of mission. What was the result? Verse 20 tells us:

> So the man went away and began to tell in the De-
> capolis how much Jesus had done for him. And all the
> people were amazed.

Mission accomplished.

The demon-possessed man is a "type" of what happens in our lives. God liberates us from sin, we stand new and fresh in Jesus, we gratefully declare our loyalty to Him, and He sends us on mission. Living on mission is not an option for His disciples. He makes this very clear in John 20:21: "As the Father has sent me, even so I am sending you" (also see John 17:18). We are all sent ones.

A mission in its simplest terms is an "assignment." I believe there is a macro mission and a micro mission that God assigns us to do. God's macro mission is the big cosmic plan for redemption—uniting all things in Christ (Eph. 1:10). He invites us to join Him in this macro mission by bringing kingdom values into the everyday places of our lives—our work, neighborhoods, apartments, and so on. His micro mission is exemplified in the demon-freed man—we are sent to start faith conversations with a neighbor.

Living on mission means entering the worlds of where we live, work, and play and inviting our adult friends to walk with us as we walk with Jesus. Mission has typically been equated with evangelism—telling others the good news of Jesus. It is this and a little bit more—it is both macro and micro. Keep reading and you will begin to see how the two work together.

As I walk in the world of adults, I've learned four lessons about living on mission. Walk with me as I walk through my life's experiences in seeking to live on mission to the world of adults.

We shine Christ's light in dark places.
We practice love rooted in place.
We take one step at a time.
We start gospel conversations.

SHINE CHRIST'S LIGHT IN DARK PLACES

Cindy began her career in an insurance company call center. She was the first voice you heard when filing an auto accident claim. As in many call centers, she had a set number of minutes per person and a quota of calls to get through per hour.

"I couldn't keep to the script," she told me. "People have just experienced a traumatic incident and they need someone to talk to. Elderly people are particularly shaken up. They're often on the phone in tears wondering what to do.

CINDY BROUGHT GOD'S KINGDOM TO WORK. SHE HELPED PEOPLE TASTE GOD'S KINGDOM BY LIVING OUT HIS VALUES IN A GIANT CORPORATION.

These conversations can't fit into a neat three-minute phone call. I decided to toss out the script and listen. This seemed to be the 'Christian thing' to do."

Was Cindy living on mission? You bet she was. Cindy was living out God's macro mission. I think of Jesus' words in the Sermon on the Mount: "You are the light of the world. A city set on a hill cannot be hidden" (Matt. 5:14). We're called to be light to dark places. Light always pushes back the darkness. How was Cindy bringing light to a dark place? What makes an insurance company a "dark" place?

Consider this particular company's governing assumptions. Efficiency trumped listening. Speed was a priority over helping people deal with tragedy. Profit overshadowed compassion.

So Cindy brought God's kingdom to work. She helped people taste God's kingdom by living out His values in a giant corporation. What values motivated her? She treated people with respect.

She listened and cared. She compassionately processed claims. She worked under the reign of kingdom values.

Cindy was committed to macro mission, influencing the culture around her in kingdom ways. She did this in a micro way, one telephone conversation at a time with each customer who needed her help.

Bringing light to dark places is important in the world of adults. Adults want to know if faith makes a difference. They want it demonstrated; they don't want to be passive listeners of a message. Our macro mission to bring light to dark places goes back to the garden.

The "garden" passages in Genesis 1–3 tell us that we're created in the "image of God." Living as lights means radiating this image into a dark world. Being an image-bearer is more than a theological statement—it's a vocation. Author and historian N. T. Wright states: "It means being called to reflect into the world the creative and redemptive love of God."[2] This is macro mission at its best.

Living as an image-bearer reminds us how ancient rulers would place statues of themselves in distant countries to remind the subject people who was ruling them. In the same way, "God has placed his own image, human beings, into his world, so that the world can see who its ruler is."[3]

You and I are those image-bearers. Into the adult routines of workplace, neighborhoods, or hobbies, God has placed His image (us!), showing what it means to be citizens of a new kingdom. "God's kingdom, inaugurated through Jesus, is all about restoring creation the way it was meant to be," and He does this "through loyal human beings,"[4] people who bear His image, people who live on mission, people who are His disciples.

Cindy was serving people at her workplace by being concerned, compassionate, and helpful. People were helped and their spirits were nourished after a phone call with her. This is macro mission in ordinary places. She was bringing in the "big picture" of God's kingdom values to an everyday setting. She was restoring a workplace to the way God intended it.

Macro mission is what author Gabe Lyons describes as those who "see themselves on a mission, partnering with God to breathe justice and mercy and peace and compassion and generosity into the world."[5] In *The New Parish*, the authors describe mission as: "bearing witness to the love of Jesus and the reign of God. It is joining the Spirit's movement in the neighborhood and seeking the reconciliation and renewal of all things."[6]

Macro mission embraces Colossians 1:19–20:

> For in him all the fullness of God was pleased to dwell,
> and through him to reconcile to himself all things,
> whether on earth or in heaven, making peace by the
> blood of his cross.

The gospel now becomes a big message; a message offering more than an "escape from hell" card. In describing the gospel of our first- and second-century church leaders, historian Michael Green writes:

> Their gospel was big enough to embrace earth and
> heaven, this life and the next. They were concerned
> with labour relations, slavery, marriage and the family,
> the exposure of children, cruelty in the amphitheatre
> and obscenity on stage. . . . There was no dichotomy

between a social and a spiritual gospel to those who held a unitive concept of truth.[7]

This is macro mission in ordinary places; this is bringing light to dark places; this is influencing our surroundings with kingdom values.

What difference does this make in an adult's life routine? Let me tell the story of Devin.

Devin was a friend from church whom I invited to read the Bible with me. As we met, read the Bible, and talked, the conversation would frequently return to his job. As an adult he spent forty-plus hours a week as a public school teacher and a supervisor of teachers. We talked about what it means to push back the darkness and bring in the light in the classroom.

"Do you have a vision for extending the kingdom at your job?" I asked. We then brainstormed on what values he would like to bring into his school, trusting God to build kingdom values into his school's culture. He gave me permission to share his vision statement:

> God willing, I will give teachers the freedom to do their jobs well while alleviating frustrations by developing relationships and integrating integrity, compassion, servanthood, and worth of individuals into my daily tasks.

In a public school, Devin is pushing back the darkness and bringing in the light of God's values. He listens to the teachers he supervises, discerning their needs. He is their advocate, securing the resources necessary for success. He represents his students to the administration, knowing that the students are the reason for the school. He is living on mission—the macro mission of bringing God's values to his workplace. Wouldn't you want Devin to be your supervisor?

LET'S SUMMARIZE MACRO MISSION:

Live among people as God's representatives
Breathe kingdom values into the world
Embrace this life and the next
Seek reconciliation and renewal of all things

Bringing light to dark places means wearing bifocal glasses. One lens is macro mission while the other is micro mission. When I invite people to walk with me on mission, I'm inviting them to both a macro and a micro way of living. Both lenses are important to see through. We can't have one without the other. We keep them in tension just as the Bible keeps them in tension. God is redeeming the cosmos while at the same time sending us to share His mercies with those in our worlds. Macro and micro go together.

How did Cindy's work review go? She had some of the highest customer evaluations in her group. Cindy ended up getting a promotion.

PRACTICE LOVE ROOTED IN PLACE

When I was a campus missionary, my "neighbor" was a twenty-year-old college student living in a dorm. As I aged and the students seemed to get younger, these "neighbors" became artificial relationships. Because I was so focused on campus ministry, I did little to relate to my actual neighbors—the adult men and women who lived on the same block that I did.

Until a few years ago, I had never combined the Great Commandment to love my neighbor with the Great Commission of making disciples. It dawned on me one day that God's simple assignment was to love my neighbor. Now, loving people means having a relationship with them. We don't love from a distance, but we love in a place—a neighborhood, workplace, family, or hobby network. Loving in place starts by building relationships.

Who is my neighbor? The etymology of the word means "a nearby dweller." I describe neighbors or a neighborhood as a place of sustained relationships where we build a shared history around a common geography or shared interest. The key to this description is that it's a place of "sustained relationships" and a "shared history."

Neighbors are people with whom we're building ongoing relationships through ongoing conversations. A neighborhood may be a city block, an apartment building, my workplace, or the local chapter of the Ohio State alumni. Neighborhoods are places where I can love the same people over a period of time. It's a place where we know one another's history and we create a shared history because we're rooted in a place and a time. Neighbors create and share a history together.

Research shows that our carefully planned evangelistic events account for

TIME AFTER TIME, WE FOUND THAT CHURCH ACTIVITIES AND VOLUNTEER RESPONSIBILITIES KEEP PEOPLE FROM TIME NEEDED TO BUILD FRIENDSHIPS.

only 10 percent of the church's conversions. In contrast, fully 85 percent of all converts come to Christ through their relationship with family and friends.[8] This powerful statistic shows the impact that everyday relationships have in bringing people to faith. Loving our neighbors is a simple strategy for living on mission.

Because friendships are critical to obeying the Great Commandment, my friend Tyler Flynn and I created a seminar we called *Making Friends for Heaven's Sake*.[9] The goal of the seminar is to help people love others in their "neighborhoods" for the sake of the gospel.

In our seminar, we ask people to schedule when they will spend time with people where they live, work, or play. We've taught this seminar to hundreds of people and in dozens of churches. Do you know what we've discovered with this assignment?

The vast majority of attendees have no significant relationships with people outside the faith. Second, they do not have time to develop relationships. One participant discovered that he had one free evening in the next month to do something with a neighbor. Do you know what occupied his other nights? Church activities.

Time after time, we found that church activities and volunteer responsibilities keep people from time needed to build friendships. If we do have free time, we're too exhausted to extend ourselves. We're like the rest of suburban America—once the garage door goes down, we don't go outside. How can we love people if we're not with people? How will people feel loved if we're not in relationship with them?

Author John Stott describes life as a good neighbor rooted in place:

It comes more natural to us to shout the gospel at
people from a distance than to involve ourselves deeply
in their lives, to think ourselves into their culture and
their problems, and to feel with them in their pains.[10]

Unlike the mindset we often see today, "the early church understood itself as *in* its place."[11] The New Testament assumes that we
live among people, rooted in a particular place, not "shouting the
gospel from a distance" but entering into the crises, conflicts, and
celebrations of people's lives (1 Thess. 1:7; 4:11–12; Col. 4:5–6).

Banned from synagogues and public gatherings, these small
groups of believers met in homes, a natural setting for relationships (Acts 2:46; Rom. 16:5). This means living in a "place" where
people see and feel the gospel in our daily lives. Being rooted
means that we stay put and pay attention to people's lives; we
share and create a history together.

The early church practiced the value of place. The third-century
Christian apologist Tertullian pointed out that Christians in his
time and place were not segregated from those around them:

We live together with you in this world, including
the forum, including the meat market, baths, shops,
workrooms, inns, fairs, and the rest of commercial
intercourse, and we sail along with you and serve in the
army and are active in agriculture and trade.[12]

To love my neighbor means I live in the same world as my
neighbor. We live, work, or play among lost people so that we can
love lost people.

Living in place means gathering with other believers who see this common place as their mission. We become a "church" in a place, gathering together in a neighborhood, workplace, or dormitory to love our neighbors. May I say it again? Living on mission is not a singles match but a team sport. Here is Ken and Linda's story.

Ken and Linda are on mission to love their neighbors. They practice loving in a place—a middle-class suburb of a midwestern city. Being rooted in place means knowing the names of the families of all ten houses on their block. One of Ken's basic neighboring principles is asking others for help. Whether it's the use of a gardening tool or assistance with a weekend job, Ken is always inviting people to help him, and people are quick to respond.

Ken and Linda soon found another neighbor who shared a faith in Christ.

As these couples served their neighbors, faith conversations naturally started. Ken, Linda, and the other Christian couple invited people to read the Bible with them. Later, when Ken was recovering from major surgery, who brought meals and helped with his recovery? His neighbors did. Ken and Linda and their team had created a place of shared history.

When Ken and Linda moved to another city to be near their children and grandchildren, this small gospel movement did not stop. Those living on mission minister together rather than as a bunch of lone rangers, which was demonstrated when the Christian couple they had recruited continued the Bible reading group with their neighbors.

Ken and Linda lived on mission in a place. This mission was simple: love people where you live, trust God for a team of like-minded people, and start faith conversations. We don't need to go overseas or engage in "stranger evangelism." We need to love people where we live. Living on mission starts with asking those outside of the faith to walk with me as I walk with Jesus.

How can we get started? Here are some simple principles Peggy and I have learned to love people in a place.

Take the initiative. Most people aren't looking for new friends. The burden is frequently on us to initiate with others. Do something simple to introduce yourself to a neighbor or coworker. Learn the names of the people in the houses around you.

Extend hospitality. You don't need to invite people to a seven-course meal. Something as simple as coffee together or ice cream on the deck starts a friendship.

Expect differences. As Neil Cole writes in *Organic Church*, "If you want to win this world to Christ, you are going to have to sit in the smoking section."[13] Jesus demonstrated how to be insulated from the world but not isolated from its people. Expect differences in language, interests, and values . . . and keep loving people.

Find common ground. We have a lot in common with our unbelieving neighbors. We battle weeds in the yard, we have children in the same school, we're trying to lose a few extra pounds, we love the Ohio State Buckeyes. We build relationships by finding common ground.

Serve. Look for ways to serve neighbors. Shovel the sidewalk after a snowstorm, mow the yard if someone is sick, or offer a kind word when crisis happens.

TAKE ONE STEP AT A TIME

The opportunity seemed right as Leo and I sat at the restaurant bar. We were meeting to plan an event for an organization we belong to. We knew each other well enough to joke and to have some serious moments. I decided to pop the question.

"Everyone has a faith story, a God story in their life. Tell me about your God story, Leo."

A simple question opened up the world of Leo's inner life. He talked about his relationship with his father and how his death impacted him at an early age. He described his frustration with the church to answer questions and how he ultimately left formal Christianity. He told me how his wife brought an element of faith back into his life and he was thinking again about God.

Everyone has a God story. In some lives, God appears very small or even nonexistent. In other lives, He's the prominent player. For many, God is a welcoming presence. For others, He's someone to shun or ignore. Everyone has a God story.

Why is this important to know? One of the lessons I've learned with adults is that sharing the good news is a process. When I live on mission with people, I need to discover where people are in this spiritual process and move them forward one step at a time. Not everyone is at the same starting point. This is at the heart of micro mission.

Discovering a person's God story tells us several things:

What do they think about God?
What do they know about Jesus?

How is eternity determined?

How do they view the Bible?

Taking one step at a time means partnering with the Holy Spirit to move people from **interest** to **insight** to **conviction**. The Holy Spirit is already working in people's lives. We need to discern where they are in the process toward becoming a new creation in Christ (2 Cor. 5:17) and join in with what He's doing. While a process is not explicitly taught in the Bible, there is biblical evidence for the progression and practical experience backs it up. Taking people one step at a time is living on micro mission.

Jesus assumes that there are periods of sowing and reaping in people's lives (John 4:35–37). Since the micro ministry of the gospel in a life is a process, not everyone is ready for the harvest. Our role is to be alert and ready, being sensitive to where a person is on the journey to Christ.

Paul understood the principle of interest. A group of Athenians heard about a new teacher in the public square and asked him to "Come and tell us about this new teaching" (Acts 17:19 NLT). They were curious about these "strange ideas he's picked up" (v. 18 NLT) and gave him an audience. Paul accepted the invitation and built on their interest.

Raising interest is what Paul calls making "the teaching about God our Savior attractive" (Titus 2:10 NLT). Making something "attractive" is like arranging jewels to display their beauty.[14] Our lives beautify the gospel, creating an interest about the Savior.

Here are some simple ways to raise people's interests:

- Raise the faith flag early. In relevant and sensitive ways, identify with Christ.
- Reference a meaningful insight from a Christian book or message.
- Share a simple "faith story" of how your faith made a difference in an everyday experience.
- Describe how you're trusting God for a difficult situation.

Interest aims to tantalize, to whet the appetite of our friends to explore Jesus.

As we spark interest, we partner with the Spirit to create insight. Consider the example of Jesus with the woman at the well. Jesus masterfully turned the conversation from asking for a drink of water to a discussion on "living water" (John 4:1–42). She realizes that this man is more than a run-of-the-mill rabbi. He could be "the Messiah—the one who is called Christ" (see John 4:25). She returns to her village with a fresh insight on the nature of the Messiah.

A simple way to lead people to insight is inviting them to read the Bible with you. (We'll discuss this in greater detail in the next section, "Start gospel conversations.") When we engage people with a firsthand experience with the Scriptures, we open the door for the Holy Spirit to give insight.

Here are some practical ways to create insight:

- Share your personal faith story.
- Invite a seeking friend to a Bible reading group.

- Invite your friend to a relevant event at church, such as a Christmas Eve concert.
- Pass on a Christian book, blog post, or website related to an issue of concern or a question he or she has.

As people move from interest to insight, we pray for **conviction**. This is the moment when the Holy Spirit convicts someone of sin, righteousness, and judgment (John 16:8). The classic example of someone coming to conviction is the Ethiopian government official in Acts 8.

The itinerant church leader Philip hears the official reading from the prophet Isaiah. Philip asks a simple question, "Do you understand what you are reading?" (Acts 8:30). The official's reply is one we all want to hear: "How can I, unless someone guides me?" (v. 31). He urges Philip to join him and explain the passage. Talk about a divine appointment! The official believes and requests immediate baptism. Conviction had occurred.

WITH THE HOLY SPIRIT'S HELP, WE CAN MOVE PEOPLE TOWARD EMBRACING JESUS ONE STEP AT A TIME.

We long for those moments of conviction, but most of the time we partner with the Holy Spirit to create interest and insight, moving people along one step at a time. We are sowing while others may reap, as we saw in John 4. When someone "reaps" it is because someone else sowed—someone moved the friend from interest to insight. Jesus honors not only the experience of conversion but the behind-the-scenes work of taking the time to love a neighbor, entering into a neighbor's joys or sorrows, and bringing a small word of faith. These ordinary acts of interest and insight set up the opportunity for another to reap.

Living on mission means trusting God for people to take one faith-step at a time—moving from interest to insight to conviction. This is a mission all of us can do. With the Holy Spirit's help, we can move people toward embracing Jesus one step at a time. This is living on micro mission.

START GOSPEL CONVERSATIONS

I get a lot of mail—several Christian magazines and a good amount of material from many Christian organizations fill my mailbox. As I greeted the mail carrier one day, he commented: "You get a lot of religious mail. What do you do, anyway?"

"I work with a Christian organization that helps leaders bring their faith values into their everyday lives. I help people live out their faith in their jobs and in their homes."

"I used to have faith," he replied. "Then I went to college and took a Bible-as-literature class and concluded that the Bible was full of errors and my faith wasn't needed. I walked away from college without a faith in God."

Here was a Holy Spirit moment. When was the last time you had a spiritual conversation with your mail carrier? I knew he was on a tight schedule so I had just a minute or two to reply. What would I say?

"I had the exact opposite happen to me. I went to college having no interest in God. I met some students who claimed to be Christians and got me reading the Bible. I found Jesus' words pretty compelling and true. I made a decision my sophomore year to follow Christ and it changed the course of my life."

"That's interesting," he replied. He then said goodbye and moved on to the next house. He retired soon after our conversation, and we never talked again.

What happened in this brief conversation? The mail carrier opened the door for conversation. Was I prepared to step into this door or would I mutter something about believing the Bible and rush inside to grab a tract?

I make a point to always be prepared for gospel conversations. I take 1 Peter 3:15 (NIV) to heart:

> Be prepared to give an answer to everyone who asks
> you to give the reason for the hope that you have. But
> do this with gentleness and respect.

I have carefully thought through my faith story, adapting it to a variety of settings. When the mail carrier opened a door, I was ready to step into his life with my story. I only had one or two minutes, since the man had a schedule to keep.

At a micro level, we must be prepared to do what author and pastor John Stott writes: "[evangelize] to him Jesus" (see Acts 8:35).[15] Jesus is the core of the gospel message. We want to talk about Jesus in the shared relationships we have with our neighbors, coworkers, and friends. At a micro level, one-to-one, we start gospel conversations.

When we look carefully at Paul's evangelism style, we notice that he debated with his audience, hearing and answering their objections (Acts 17:1–4). His approach was one of reasoning and dialogue with his hearers, whether with groups or with individuals.[16] Engagement through dialogue, argumentation, and question-and-answer sessions marked Paul's evangelism. Conversing about the gospel didn't stop with the apostle.

The gospel spread through the Roman Empire in the early centuries not through public preaching but through conversations about Jesus. Historian Robin Fox writes, "We have no historical text which refers to formal, open-air sermons outside a church after the mid first-century."[17] In fact, the word "merchant"—those sellers who traveled the popular trade routes—became "a metaphor for those who spread the gospel."[18] The gospel traveled the routes of natural relationships carried by everyday people.

Church historian Michael Green describes it this way:

> This [evangelizing] must often have been not formal preaching, but the informal chattering to friends and chance acquaintances, in homes and wine shops, on walks, and around market stalls. They went everywhere gossiping the gospel; they did it naturally, enthusiastically, and with the conviction of those who are not paid to say that sort of thing. Consequently, they were taken seriously.[19]

What's fascinating is that the original telling of the Christian message was a two-way conversation. Then something happened. When the oratorical schools of the West took hold of the Christian message, preaching became something different from a conversation. Oratory—skilled public speaking—replaced conversation. The eloquence of the speaker superseded Jesus and

His resurrection. The dialogue between speaker and listener soon became a monologue.[20]

Conversations connect with adults. My peers aren't inviting me to preach a sermon. They want to talk.

Here are three simple ways we can encourage gospel conversations at a micro level.

1. We tell our story.
2. We invite others to explore His story through a Bible-reading group.
3. We tell His story.

We Tell Our Story

Adults love personal stories. We constantly seek out "testimonials." The first thing I do before I make a major purchase is read the online reviews. I want to know firsthand how others have experienced the product. Our story about Jesus is a testimonial about a "product's" usefulness.

My testimony or faith story puts into words what God has done in my life, creating a door-opener for extended faith conversations. A faith story builds bridges to the souls of others who have similar questions, deep hurts, or desired hopes. A testimony is not a "convincing" tool but a cultivating tool to create interest or give insight.

Here are some marks of a good testimony:

- It is no longer than two or three minutes.
- It isn't filled with Christianese terms such as "saved," "sin," "righteousness," "reconciled." (The list could go on. Most unbelievers are not familiar with these words.)

- It isn't a talk about church or a disparagement of other religions.
- It is centered on Christ. He is the one who changed your life, not a church service or minister.
- It focuses on specifics for how Christ has changed and is changing your life now. Adults want to know "if this faith stuff works."

Invite Others to Read His Story

"I didn't realize that Jesus had His own posse! That's pretty cool." This was Scott's observation about Jesus as we read and discussed the gospel of Mark. Scott was in a group of ten men who gathered Friday mornings in an office boardroom to read the Bible and talk about Jesus. Seven of the ten men were seekers. They had an interest, and this small group provided the insight.

This was not a Bible study or a Bible teaching time. We had a list of questions that prompted discussion. In fact, we rotated the group's facilitation to include believers and unbelievers. After all, we followed the same set of questions from week to week so anyone could ask the questions. Our goal was to read the Gospels and let Jesus do the talking.

The format was simple: we looked at the text and made observations about Jesus. The prepared discussion questions kept us on track and forced the participants to observe the text carefully rather than speculate about its meaning. A Bible-reading group allows people to directly encounter Jesus in His Word.

Adults want to talk, question, and explore. They want dialogue to come up with their own answers. A Bible reading group invites people into a discussion about Jesus through His words. It is not a teaching time but a discussion around the Scriptures. Here are some simple principles for facilitating a Bible reading group:

- Form a small team. Ask several Christian friends to invite interested friends to explore the Scriptures in a small group.
- Hold down the number of believers. Too many Christians turns it into a Sunday school class and limits the participation of the unbelievers.
- Focus on those who believe differently, not those who share our beliefs. Compile a list of interested people, pray, and invite.
- Don't teach but discuss. Have a common set of questions that everyone has access to.
- Let Jesus do the talking. Focus on the text and what Jesus is doing and saying. Let His example and teaching penetrate people's hearts.

Through reading and discussing the Gospels, first Matt came to faith, and then a young executive named Eric embraced the Savior. Inviting people to read the Bible builds on one's interests and gives insight, which the Holy Spirit uses to convict.[21]

The goal of the Bible reading group is to engage interested friends in a firsthand encounter with Jesus in the Scriptures. Remember, we want to let Jesus do the talking.[22]

Tell His Story

"Every day I try to do something good for someone. Isn't this what the Golden Rule teaches? God has to notice my choices."

Michael's statement caught me by surprise. Here was an open door for a conversation and I was caught flat-footed. While I thought about how to answer, the moment was gone and Michael was on to another topic.

What saved this conversation was the fact that we're friends and I could go back to this conversation at another time. About two weeks later the opportunity arose.

"Remember your comment about the Golden Rule and helping others? You do a great job of this, Mike. There's not many people I know who help others like you do. But the Bible says that the amount of good that I do is not the way to heaven."

I'VE LEARNED TWO SIMPLE LESSONS. THE FIRST SOUNDS LIKE A BROKEN RECORD: EVANGELISM IS AN ONGOING CONVERSATION.

Knowing that Michael was a sports fan, I asked him, "Have you ever seen the guy at football games with John 3:16 on his shirt or on a sign he holds up? That's probably a verse that everyone knows." I then repeated the verse and added, "God says eternal life is assured by believing in Christ, not in the good we do." Michael nodded and moved on.

Living on mission with Michael means having repeated conversations about spiritual things. I want to keep the conversation going. I want to keep moving the ball of Jesus down the field toward the goal line of his conversion.

In telling His story, the good news of the gospel, I've learned two simple lessons. The first sounds like a broken record: evangelism is an ongoing conversation. I want to bring up Jesus again and again in multiple ways.

Second, I want to explain the gospel in simple and understandable ways, omitting the Christian verbiage we're so familiar with. Our Christian words can sound like a foreign language to our unchurched friends. Here's a humorous example from my friend Cliff.

> Kent came up to me the other day at work and told me that he was thinking about his finances. He had seen this billboard that said "Jesus saves!" "I didn't realize that Jesus was into banking," he said. "Maybe if someone as important as Jesus thinks about saving I should do the same."

This is a true story! It shows us that how we explain the gospel needs to be in everyday words and examples, and also not to overuse Christian jargon that can easily be misunderstood.

We explain the gospel in conversational and relevant approaches. While I value tracts or pamphlets, I use them as a last resort. I prefer to sow the gospel in bits and pieces, using the Scriptures and real-world examples to convey the message.[23] This is living on micro mission.

LET'S SUMMARIZE MICRO MISSION:

Love our neighbors
Partner with the Holy Spirit to move people from interest to insight to conviction
Start faith conversations

TO WRAP UP: YARDENING

"Yardening" has been called the number one hobby in the United States. Yardening is a combination of gardening and caring for a yard. More people "yarden" in the US than any other hobby.

Peggy and I are avid yardeners. Peggy is a certified Master Gardener and I'm the guy who digs the holes! We have a vision for our small plot of land. We want to create a spot of beauty in a dark world, a space where people can sense the creative presence of God. How committed are yardeners like us?

In Ohio, the frost date is typically around May 15. By this time it's safe to plant without the fear of frost. If the date falls close to a weekend, nurseries and garden centers are besieged by people like us. One popular garden center hires a policeman to direct traffic in and out of the lot. Talk about fanaticism!

Standing in line one mid-May, with a shopping cart filled with annuals and perennials, I looked around at the other three lines of people waiting to pay. I thought about how this nursery is selling plants to be planted in every corner of our community. The nursery's mission is to get rid of plants, not to keep plants. Soon their products will be planted in hundreds, and probably thousands, of homes scattered around Columbus.

With this simple revelation, my mind drifted back to Peggy's and my recent visit to the Franklin Park and Conservatory in Columbus. We love going to the conservatory in mid-winter. The conservatory doesn't get rid of plants; it keeps and exhibits plants. We wander from the bonsai room, to the desert room, to the tropical rain forest room, to the orchid room. Plants are looked at, photographed, and enjoyed within an artificial environment.

Then my mind took an odd turn. I asked myself this: *Which of these two places should the church be like? Should our mission be like the conservatory, preserving plants (people) in an artificial setting? Or should our mission be like the garden center, getting rid of our plants by planting them in every corner of the community?*

I think you can guess the answer. The local church should be like a garden center. Our mission is to grow plants (people), not to put them on display in a safe setting, but to release them to be planted in every corner of a community. The sad reality is that many churches are more like a conservatory, keeping and protecting people, putting them on display to be admired but not planted in the harsh realities of life outside the building.

When we choose the route of the garden center, we choose to live on mission. Mission means inviting people to walk with us as we walk with Jesus. We put on our bifocal glasses and live out our mission in macro and micro ways. This means bringing light to dark places, practicing love rooted in place, helping people take one step at a time, and starting gospel conversations. The goal is the same with a seeker or a believer—walk with me as I walk with Jesus.

WALK ON MISSION

SHINE CHRIST'S LOVE IN DARK PLACES

Put on bifocal glasses
Practice macro mission
Live micro mission

PRACTICE LOVE ROOTED IN PLACE

Take initiative
Expect differences
Find commom ground
Serve

TAKE ONE STEP AT A TIME

Move people from
interest to
insight to
conviction

START GOSPEL CONVERSATIONS

Tell my story
Explore His story in the Bible
Tell His story

CHAPTER SIX

LIVE THE JOY

Joy is the business of heaven.

C. S. LEWIS

I've been a member of Weight Watchers for some time now. I constantly fight the "battle of the bulge," and this discipline gives me victory in weight loss.

To get started, Weight Watchers leaders emphasize the importance of "finding your why." Your "why" is your vision, your inner motivation for weight loss. This "why" sustains me when I want to gobble a bag of potato chips or guzzle a liter of pop. Just as we need a "why" for weight loss, so we need one for making disciples.

Inviting people to walk with us as we walk with Jesus is challenging. It's work to keep going when people miss discipleship times, when they call at inconvenient hours, or when they make poor life decisions. Relationships take a lot of effort. It's much easier for people to just attend a class.

When I want to quit and go back to the old ways of curriculums and programs instead of relationships, I have to come back to my "why." Why do I want to invest in a people strategy that starts small and goes slow? Why do I want to invest in a ministry that is often heartbreaking and requires emotional work? Why would I invite someone to walk with me? A conversation with my friend Rich affirmed again why both of us want to make disciples. The story he told me about Ben captures a "why."

Ben is a former alcoholic. Through a series of events, Rich befriended Ben and shared his faith story. Ben came to faith. Here was a man in his mid-sixties whose life was changed by Jesus. He overcame his alcohol addiction and made real strides in his Christian walk.

Ben volunteered to help Rich's church in their service at a homeless shelter. While at this shelter, he befriended a man who was having trouble forgiving certain individuals. Ben knew what that felt like and invited the man to read the Bible with him. Ben had never done this before. In fact, in his wildest dreams he never imagined himself doing such a thing. But just as Rich had come alongside him, Ben is now coming alongside another friend to read the Bible. Every week Rich would suggest some new verses for Ben to use in his discussion with his new friend.

"A life change like Ben's affirms that the gospel is real," I said in response to Rich's story.

"You bet it does!" was Rich's reply.

Organizing one more program, promoting one more event, or teaching one more class will tire anyone after a while. I only have so much energy to expend for this routine. However, if I'm investing my life's energies in people—inviting them to walk with me as Jesus' disciples—then joy happens, and my why becomes activated.

Paul understood this joy. He rhetorically asks, "What is our hope or joy or crown of boasting . . . ? Is it not you?" (1 Thess. 2:19).

The Thessalonians were his joy because he was emotionally and relationally invested in them.

These men and women received more than a verbal gospel message from him. Paul gave them of himself (1 Thess. 2:8). People were not ministry projects, numbers in a worship service, or giving units. Paul knew them as friends. He had invited them to walk with him as he walked with Jesus.

When we're relationally invested in people's lives, we know how God is changing them. We hear the stories about when they share their faith, and we praise God when they turn from sinful habits to love Him (1 Thess. 1:8–9). We brag about their generosity to others (2 Cor. 9:2).

OUR "MEANS" ARE THE BIBLE STUDIES, CONVERSATIONS, OR PRACTICAL SEMINARS THAT MAKE UP THE PATH TO MATURITY. WHILE IT'S PLEASURABLE TO COUNT ATTENDANCE, THE MOST SATISFYING "END" IS ALWAYS A CHANGED LIFE FOR JESUS' GLORY.

This kind of intimate knowledge is learned not from a casual conversation between church services or in an email exchange. We hear these stories because we're investing in people one-to-one, one-to-two, or one-to-three—we're practicing small circle disciplemaking. When we emotionally invest in people, we hear and see God at work firsthand—and we give Him the glory for it.

Joy happens when God is glorified. Now we have found our why.

To wrap up, remember "means" and "ends." Make your "end" the apostle John's goal: "I have no greater joy than to hear that my children are walking in the truth" (3 John 4). The "children" in this passage are John's spiritual children, not his physical children. The joy of seeing his children mature, walking in God's truth, was John's why, his end.

Our "means" are the Bible studies, conversations, or practical seminars that make up the path to maturity. While it's pleasurable to count attendance, the most satisfying "end" is always a changed life for Jesus' glory. This is the greatest thrill we can have—the thrill of seeing the gospel transform a life. This is what gets me out of bed each morning. I have found my "why."

This book is littered with people who are our friends, people Peggy and I have invited to walk with us as we walk with Jesus. Todd, Glenn, Kim, Christy, Dan, Stan, Amanda, and others fill the pages. Behind their changed names and slightly altered circumstances stand real people with whom we had real conversations. These men and women are our friends.

Each one is our joy. Each story represents a changed life, a little slice of history that stands to glorify God. What a privilege to have a small role in helping them follow Jesus.

May the Lord help you find His joy in people. Joy happens when we invite people to walk with us as we walk with Jesus. Joy happens as we live heart-to-heart with people, keeping the faith simple, going slow, growing deep, and living on mission. When we practice these principles, we will experience the joy of seeing our Lord change lives. When people become your why, you will live the joy . . . and God will get the glory!

WHAT HAPPENS NEXT?

My friend Monty is a life and leadership coach. He has a saying about change: "Nothing has really happened until it's on the calendar." In other words, talk is cheap until we do something about it.

Jesus expressed change in a word picture:

> "Everyone who comes to me and hears my words and
> does them, I will show you what he is like: he is like
> a man building a house, who dug deep and laid the
> foundation on the rock."
> —*Luke 6:47–48*

The house that stands is the house built on the rock of obedience. You now have a choice to make. Will you simply savor the memory of reading this book? Or will you take some action on what you discovered? Now is the time to invite others to "walk with me as I walk with Jesus." How do you start walking?

1. ***Be available.*** The one "ability" God is looking for is our "availability." Are you available for the Lord to use you to disciple some men and women? What do you need to change in your schedule to make time to invest in people?

2. **Pray.** Jesus spent the night in prayer before He chose the Twelve (Luke 6:12). You may not spend an entire night, but you can begin to pray. Ask God to connect you with men and women who "show up" and who want to grow.

3. **Look.** Look around your network of relationships. This can include your place of work, where you live, your church, Sunday school class, campus ministry, fitness club, and so on. Who are the believers around you who show up to grow and who need someone to come alongside them to learn to live the disciple's life?

4. **Invite.** Prayerfully settle on two or three people for a small circle of discipleship. If you can't identify two or three people, ask God for one. Check out the suggestions on inviting in chapter 2.

5. **Start where they are.** Take some time to identify where someone is on their discipleship journey. Draw out The Navigators Wheel and ask him or her which spoke is the longest and which is the shortest. If meeting with a small circle, decide on an appropriate discipleship course of study. Some excellent selections are:

   - The Navigators *2:7 Series* (read about this and order from www.navigators.org/resource/the-27-seriesnavpress.com)
   - *Every Man a Warrior* (everymanawarrior.com)
   - *A Woman's Guide to Discipling* (read about this and order from www.navigators.org/resource/a-womans-guide-to-discipling/)
   - High Quest (highquest.info)

6. ***Think deep.*** Don't just take people through a study, but be thinking about how you will go deep with the people in your discipleship circle. Employ the principles of heart, head, hands, helps, and habits from chapter 4.

7. ***Practice heart-to-heart.*** Remember, this is a relationship, not a program. A simple way to go heart-to-heart is to ask people to draw a time line of their faith journey, noting the people and events that shaped their lives. Share this timeline with one another. Give people plenty of time to give lots of details.

8. ***Multiply.*** Be like Jesus and start the relationship with the end goal in mind (Matt. 4:19). Our goal in this group/relationship is not to absorb this for ourselves but to pass on what we're learning to another. We want to invite others to walk with us as we walk with Jesus. Multiplication means one disciple making a disciple who makes a disciple.

What happens next? Be available to the Lord and see what He will do. Let's start walking!

ACKNOWLEDGMENTS

Behind any author are friends who supported, encouraged, and modeled the things that the author writes about. I could not have authored this book without my wife Peggy's support. She gave up evenings and weekends together for me to write. Her love, support, and belief in my calling to write has been invaluable. I love you, Peggy!

Second, I need to thank my friend Ed. Without his initial invitation to read the Bible with him in the study lounge, I would not be here today. Thank you, Ed! By the way, at seventy years old, Ed is still discipling men.

Like many authors, I'm appreciative of the editors at Moody Publishers. Thanks Duane Sherman for enthusiastically supporting this book and providing the guidance to keep it simple and focused. Thanks Pam Pugh for providing all the detail work and tracking down several of the quotes to their original sources.

Finally, I want to thank The Navigators. God has used this organization to not only give me a life purpose, but friends in this ministry have modeled this life of "walk with me as I walk with Jesus." Faithful friends and leaders have shaped me as a person and my ministry philosophy. In particular, I want to thank the Great Lakes Regional staff team who encouraged me to write.

Thank you, Dane, Nate, Lou, Patti, Jack, and Justin. I also want to thank my friend Randy who taught me so much about asking questions. My life is richer because of these men and women.

TEN BOOKS TO INFLAME YOUR HEART FOR GOD

Brother Lawrence, *The Practice of the Presence of God* (public domain; many versions are readily available).

Wayne Cordeiro, *The Divine Mentor: Growing Your Faith as You Sit at the Feet of the Savior* (Bloomington, MN: Bethany, 2007).

Jean Fleming, *Feeding Your Soul: A Quiet Time Handbook* (Colorado Springs: NavPress, 1999).

Richard Foster, *The Celebration of Discipline: Special Anniversary Edition* (Grand Rapids: HarperOne, 2018).

Jan Johnson, *Enjoying the Presence of God: Discovering Intimacy with God in the Daily Rhythms of Life* (Colorado Springs: NavPress, 1996).

Charles Swindoll, *Intimacy with the Almighty* (Nashville: J. Countryman Press, 1999).

Eugene Peterson, *Answering God: The Psalms as Tools for Prayer* (New York: HarperOne, 1991).

A. W. Tozer, *The Pursuit of God* (Chicago: Moody, 2015).

Ann Voskamp, *One Thousand Gifts: A Dare to Live Fully Right Where You Are* (Grand Rapids: Zondervan, 2011).

Dallas Willard, *Hearing God: Developing a Conversational Relationship with God* (Downers Grove, IL: InterVarsity, 2012).

PUTTING
FIRST THINGS FIRST

In his book *Intimacy with the Almighty,* author and pastor Chuck Swindoll writes that for many, "intimacy with the Almighty remains a distant dream." This should not be so. Our Lord invites us into a relationship with Him. He calls it a "fellowship" (1 Cor. 1:9), a "friendship" (John 15:15), and a "first love" (Rev. 2:4 NASB).

Like any relationship, we must practice some simple habits for it to grow and flourish. Relationships do not happen without intentionality, time, and commitment. A simple practice to grow our "first love" is a daily time with God.

Over the years, a variety of words have been used to describe this time—a daily watch, a devotional, a quiet time. Whatever term we use, the practice is the same. We intentionally set aside time each day to come into our Lord's presence, put aside our agendas to listen to Him through His Word, and respond back to Him in prayer.

Whether it's for ten minutes, thirty minutes, or an hour, this time is set aside to build our friendship with God. What do we do in this time? Here are some simple practices.

Renew. Stop to renew your heart for God. This can happen by expressing our wonder for Him in worship or confessing our sins of disobedience. We stop to renew our hearts. *Lord, how can I praise You today? Lord, what actions have I taken that offended You?*

Read. We take time to read the Scriptures. We daily have a plan to read the Bible. *Lord, open up my head and heart to Your truth today.*

Reflect. Reflection means meditating or thinking about the Bible. We pause to think about the words, phrases, and meaning of the text. The goal is not a speed reading plan but a slow, inquisitive approach to the Bible. *Lord, give me one new thought from You today from Your Word.*

Record. We take time to record or write down what the Lord is teaching us as we reflect on His Word. *Lord, what is the one new thought or insight You gave me today?*

Respond. We first respond in prayer, praying back to God what we have reflected on in His Word. We then respond in a simple act of obedience. This application is not a lifetime commitment but a simple response to the Word that can be done in the next twenty-four hours. *Lord, what would my life look like in the next twenty-four hours if I applied the thought You gave me from Your Word?*

Repeat. We plan our next time with God. We secure a place, a time, and a friend who will help us be faithful to this practice. *Lord, give me the discipline and focus to spend time with You again tomorrow.*

The goal is not to be committed to a method but to a person. Simple disciplines build relationships. We practice a daily time with God to keep our first love renewed and refreshed. May our intimacy with the Father no longer be a dream but a reality.

These principles were drawn from my discipleship resource, *First Things First*. You can access this resource and other disciple-making tools by visiting www.alongsider.com.

NOTES

AN INVITATION

1. Eugene Peterson, *As Kingfishers Catch Fire: A Conversation on the Ways of God Formed by the Words of God* (New York: Waterbrook, 2017), 77.
2. Dallas Willard, *The Great Omission: Reclaiming Jesus's Essential Teachings on Discipleship* (New York: HarperCollins, 2006), 3.
3. George Barna, *Growing True Disciples: New Strategies for Producing Genuine Followers of Christ* (New York: Waterbrook, 2001), 38.

START WALKING

Epigraph: Timothy Keller, "Finding God in Suffering," *Relevant Magazine*, October 14, 2013, https://relevantmagazine.com/god/finding-god-suffering/.

1. This sequence was drawn from Johnston M. Cheney, *The Life of Christ in Stereo: The Four Gospels Combined as One* (Colorado Springs: Multnomah, 1984).
2. Bruce Milne, *The Message of John* (Downers Grove, IL: InterVarsity, 1993), 56.
3. William Barclay, *The Gospel of John*, vol. 1 (Louisville, KY: Westminster John Knox Press, 2001), 102.
4. Ibid.
5. You can read more about The Navigators's mission, history, and work at www.navigators.org.
6. Kenneth Boa, *Life in the Presence of God: Practices for Living in Light of Eternity* (Downers Grove, IL: InterVarsity, 2017), 20.
7. J. A. Motyer, *The Message of Philippians* (Downers Grove, IL: InterVarsity, 1984), 176–77.

8. Brennan Manning, *The Ragamuffin Gospel: Good News for the Bedraggled, Beat-up, and Burnt Out* (Colorado Springs: Multnomah, 2005), 45.

9. Wolfgang Bauder, "Disciple," in Colin Brown, gen. ed., *The New International Dictionary of New Testament Theology*, vol. 1 (Grand Rapids: Zondervan, 1980), 488.

10. Ibid., 491.

11. *Pocket Oxford English Dictionary*, 11th ed., s.v. "way" (Oxford, UK: Oxford University Press, 2013), 1050.

CHAPTER ONE: PRINCIPLE 1—
WE WALK HEART-TO-HEART

Epigraph: James M. Houston, *The Prayer: Deepening Your Friendship with God* (Colorado Springs: Cook, 2007), 204.

1. Eugene Peterson, *As Kingfishers Catch Fire: A Conversation on the Ways of God Formed by the Words of God* (New York: Waterbrook, 2017), 76.

2. Steve Garber, *Visions of Vocation: Common Grace for the Common Good* (Downers Grove, IL: InterVarsity, 2014), 123.

3. John Piper, *Think: The Life of the Mind and the Love of God* (Wheaton, IL: Crossway, 2010), 84, 86.

4. Terrence Erdt, *Jonathan Edwards: Art and the Sense of the Heart* (Amherst, MA: University of Massachusetts Press, 1980), 11.

5. Brennan Manning, *Bread and Wine: Readings for Lent and Easter* (Maryknoll, NY: Orbis Books, 2005), 224.

6. James K. A. Smith, *You Are What You Love: The Spiritual Power of Habit* (Grand Rapids: Brazos, 2016), 29. This quote is from Geoff Dyer, *Zona: A Book about a Film about a Journey to a Room* (New York: Vintage, 2012), 161.

7. Jean Fleming, *Feeding Your Soul: A Quiet Time Handbook* (Colorado Springs: NavPress, 1999), 19.

8. Jan Johnson, *Savoring God's Word: Cultivating the Soul-Transforming Practice of Scripture Meditation* (Colorado Springs: NavPress, 2004), 37.

9. Andrew Murray, *The School of Obedience*, 124. The book I have that sold for 50 cents was published by Moody Books (now Moody Publishers, which offers this classic as an e-book). You can find this highly recommended book in various formats, including with slightly updated language.

10. In Appendix B you will find a simple format for how to plan a daily time with God.

11. William Barclay, *The Letters to the Philippians, Colossians, and Thessalonians* (Louisville, KY: Westminster John Knox Press, 2003), 223.

12. Philip Yancy, *Prayer: Does It Make Any Difference?* (Grand Rapids: Zondervan, 2006), 41.

13. Bill Mowry, *The Ways of the Alongsider: Growing Disciples Life to Life* (Colorado Springs: NavPress, 2016), 53.

14. *Merriam-Webster*, s.v. "empathy," last updated November 9, 2020, https://www.merriam-webster.com/dictionary/empathy.

15. Howard Hendricks, *Teaching to Change Lives: Seven Proven Ways to Make Your Teaching Come Alive* (Colorado Springs: Multnomah, 2003), 94.

CHAPTER TWO: PRINCIPLE 2—
WE WALK SIMPLE

1. Leander Kahney, *Inside Steve's Brain* (New York: Penguin, 2008), 61–62.

2. Alan Siegel and Irene Etzkorn, *Simple: Conquering the Crisis of Complexity* (New York/Boston: Twelve, 2013), 7.

3. Robert E. Coleman, *The Master Plan of Evangelism*, 2nd ed. (Grand Rapids: Revell, 1993; Spire, 2010), 21, 26.

4. Greg McKeown, *Essentialism: The Disciplined Pursuit of Less* (New York: Crown Business, 2014), 7.

5. George Barna, *Growing True Disciples: New Strategies for Producing Genuine Followers of Christ* (Colorado Springs: WaterBrook, 2001), 8.

6. This widely cited quote by W. MacNeile Dixon from *The Human Situation* is also quoted by Warren Wiersbe in *Preaching and Teaching with Imagination* (Grand Rapids: Baker, 2007), 24.

7. Garr Reynolds, *Presentation Zen: Simple Ideas on Presentation Design and Delivery* (Berkeley, CA: New Riders, 2008), 132.

8. The Wheel © 1976 The Navigators. Used by permission. All rights reserved.

9. Esther de Waal, *Lost in Wonder: Rediscovering the Spiritual Art of Attentiveness* (Collegeville, MN: Liturgical Press, 2003), 82.

CHAPTER THREE: PRINCIPLE 3—
WE WALK SLOW

Epigraph: Dietrich Bonhoeffer, *Meditating on the Word* (Cambridge, MA: Cowley Publications, 2000), 122.

1. Thomas Friedman, *Thank You For Being Late: An Optimist's Guide to Thriving in the Age of Accelerations* (New York: Farrar Strauss Giroux, 2016), 32, 33.

2. Noga Arikha, "2010: How Is the Internet Changing the Way You Think?," Edge, www.edge.org/response-detail/26799.

3. Ann Voskamp, *One Thousand Gifts: A Dare to Live Fully Right Where You Are* (Grand Rapids: Zondervan, 2011), 67.

4. Ray Bradbury, *Fahrenheit 451* (New York: Ballantine Books, 1996), 84.

5. Christian McEwen, *World Enough & Time: On Creativity and Slowing Down* (Peterborough, NH: Bauhan, 2011), 188.

6. Ibid., 19–20.

7. Eugene Peterson, *Practice Resurrection: A Conversation on Growing Up in Christ* (Grand Rapids: Eerdmans, 2010), 133.

8. Esther de Waal, *Lost in Wonder: Rediscovering the Spiritual Art of Attentiveness* (Collegeville, MN: Liturgical Press, 2003), 87.

9. Frank E. Gaebelein, ed., *The Expositor's Bible Commentary, Colossians* (Grand Rapids: Zondervan, 1978), 216–17.

10. Oswald Chambers, *My Utmost for His Highest,* October 21 selection (Grand Rapids: Discovery House, 1927).

11. Os Guinness, *The Call: Finding and Fulfilling God's Purpose for Your Life* (Nashville: W Publishing, 2018), 250.

12. Linda Verlee Williams, *Teaching for the Two-Sided Mind: A Guide to Right Brain/Left Brain Education* (New York: Simon & Schuster, 1983), 2–3.

13. Wendell Berry, *Our Only World: Ten Essays* (Berkeley, CA: Counterpoint, 2015), 121.

14. McEwen, *World Enough & Time*, 188.

15. Wendell Berry, *The Art of the Commonplace: The Agrarian Essays of Wendell Berry* (Berkeley, CA: Counterpoint, 2002), 290.

16. Leighton Ford, *The Attentive Life: Discerning God's Presence in All Things* (Downers Grove, IL: InterVarsity, 2008), 22.

CHAPTER FOUR: PRINCIPLE 4—
WE WALK DEEP

Epigraph: Richard Foster, *Celebration of Discipline, Special Anniversary Edition* (Grand Rapids: HarperOne, 2018), 1.

1. Kenneth Boa, *Life in the Presence of God: Practices for Living in Light of Eternity* (Downers Grove, IL: InterVarsity, 2017), 128.

2. Peter Scazzero, *Emotionally Healthy Spirituality: It's Impossible to Be

Spiritually Mature While Remaining Emotionally Immature (Grand Rapids: Zondervan 2017), 191.

3. J. A, Motyer, *The Message of James* (Downers Grove, IL: InterVarsity, 1985), 41.

4. James K. A. Smith, *You Are What You Love: The Spiritual Power of Habit* (Grand Rapids: Brazos, 2016), 7.

5. Ibid., 9.

6. Robert K. Barnhart, ed., *The Barnhart Concise Dictionary of Etymology*, s.v. "inspire" (New York: Harper Collins, 1995), 391.

7. Jan Johnson, *Invitation to the Jesus Life: Experiments in Christlikeness* (Colorado Springs: NavPress, 2008), 148.

8. Robert E. Coleman, *The Master Plan of Evangelism* (Tappan, NJ: Revell, 1971), 80.

9. Dallas Willard, *The Renovation of the Heart: Putting on the Character of Christ* (Colorado Springs: NavPress, 2002), 85.

10. Ibid., 83.

11. Dallas Willard, *The Spirit of the Disciplines: Understanding How God Changes Lives* (New York: HarperCollins, 1991), 110.

12. Henri Nouwen, *Discernment: Reading the Signs of Daily Life* (New York: HarperOne, 2015), 136.

13. Ruth Haley Barton, *Sacred Rhythms: Arranging Our Lives for Spiritual Transformation* (Downers Grove, IL: InterVarsity, 2006), 12.

14. Dallas Willard, *The Great Omission: Reclaiming Jesus' Essential Teachings on Discipleship* (New York: HarperCollins, 2006), 34.

15. Richard Foster, *Celebration of Discipline, Special Anniversary Edition* (Grand Rapids: HarperOne, 2018), 7.

CHAPTER FIVE: PRINCIPLE 5—
WE WALK ON MISSION

Epigraph: Quoted in Gabe Lyons, *The Next Christians: Seven Ways You Can Live the Gospel and Restore the World* (Colorado Springs: Multnomah, 2010), 8.

1. Larry Poston, "The Adult Gospel," *Christianity Today*, January 1, 2002, www.christianitytoday.com/ct/2002/januaryweb-only/32.0.html?share=.

2. N. T. Wright, *The Challenge of Jesus: Rediscovering Who Jesus Was and Is* (Downers Grove, IL: InterVarsity, 2015), 183.

3. N. T. Wright, *After You Believe: Why Christian Character Matters* (New York: HarperCollins, 2010), 76.

4. N. T. Wright, *God and the Pandemic: A Christian Reflection on the Coronavirus and Its Aftermath* (Grand Rapids: Zondervan, 2020), 32.

5. Gabe Lyons, *The Next Christians: Seven Ways You Can Live the Gospel and Restore the World* (Colorado Springs: Multnomah, 2010), 59.

6. Paul Sparks, Tim Soerens, and Dwight J. Friesen, *The New Parish: How Neighborhood Churches Are Transforming Mission, Discipleship and Community* (Downers Grove, IL: InterVarsity, 2014), 86.

7. Michael Green, *Evangelism in the Early Church*, rev. ed. (Grand Rapids: Eerdmans, 2003), 385.

8. Research was conducted by the Church Growth Institute and cited in Walter L. Larimore and William Carr Peel, *The Saline Solution: Sharing Christ in a Busy Practice* (New York: Del Rey/Ballantine Books, 1996).

9. This seven-week study guide for groups or individuals, *Making Friends for Heaven's Sake: How to Move Casual Relationships to Spiritual Relationships* by Bill Mowry and Tyler Flynn, is available on Amazon.com.

10. John R. W. Stott, *Christian Mission in the Modern World* (Downers Grove, IL: InterVarsity, 1975), 25.

11. Sparks, Soerens, Friesen, *The New Parish*, 39.

12. Ramsay MacMullen, *Christianizing the Roman Empire: A.D. 100–400* (New Haven, CT: Yale University, 1984), 40.

13. Neil Cole, *Organic Church: Growing Faith Where Life Happens* (San Francisco: Jossey-Bass, 2005), xxvii.

14. John R. W. Stott, *Guard the Truth: The Message of 1 Timothy and Titus* (Downers Grove, IL: InterVarsity, 1996), 191.

15. Stott, *Christian Mission in the Modern World*, 44.

16. Ibid., 63.

17. Robin Lane Fox, *Pagans and Christians: In the Mediterranean World from the Second Century AD to the Conversion of Constantine* (New York: HarperCollins, 1986), 284.

18. Philip Jenkins, *The Lost History of Christianity: The Thousand-Year Golden Age of the Church in the Middle East, Africa, and Asia—and How It Died* (New York: HarperCollins, 2009), 63.

19. Green, *Evangelism in the Early Church*, 243.

20. Wayne E. Oates, *Protestant Pastoral Counseling* (Philadelphia: Westminster Press, 1962), 162; quoted in Frank Viola and George Barna, *Pagan Christianity: Exploring the Roots of Our Church Practices* (Carol Stream, IL: Tyndale, 2008), 92.

21. You can download material for leading a Bible reading group at my website: www.alongsider.com. Check out the resources tab to download "A Quickstart Guide for Leading Bible Reading Groups" and questions to lead a discussion in the gospel of John. Another excellent resource is the work of Mary Schaller and Q Place (www.qplace.com). Mary Schaller and John Crilly, *The 9 Arts of Spiritual Conversations: Walking Alongside People Who Believe Differently* (Carol Stream, IL: Tyndale, 2016).

22. You can obtain "A Quickstart Guide for Leading Bible Reading Groups" at alongsider.com.

23. An excellent tool is *One-Verse Evangelism: A Simple Way to Share the Gospel* by Randy Raysbrook and Steve Walker, or for more resources, go to: https://www.navigators.org/resource/one-verse-evangelism/.

CHAPTER SIX: LIVE THE JOY

Epigraph: C. S. Lewis, *Letters to Malcolm, Chiefly on Prayer* (New York: HarperCollins, 1963), 125.

ARE YOU DISSATISFIED WITH YOUR SPIRITUAL LIFE?

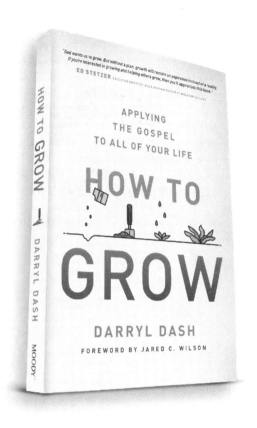

How to Grow is for people who want to grow spiritually and help others grow as well. Darryl Dash demonstrates how the gospel continues to fuel transformation in the life of every believer long after conversion. Then he walks you through a practical, habit-based approach to spiritual growth.

978-0-8024-1819-7 | also available as an eBook

HOW CAN YOU TELL IF YOU'RE ACTUALLY GROWING?

Nancy Kane explores the five stages of the soul's journey toward loving God. From stage one, first love, to stage five, intimate love, you will learn where you are, how to grow in love toward God and others, and how to embrace a faith that heals and fills you.

978-0-8024-1690-2 | also available as eBook and audiobook

A PRACTICAL GUIDE TO CREATING AND SUSTAINING A CULTURE OF DISCIPLE-MAKING IN ANY CHURCH

MOODY Publishers®

From the Word to Life®

Replicate shows church leaders how to make disciples who make disciples and get the rest of your church on board. Learn the five marks of a healthy disciple-making church, how to influence culture, uproot misconceptions of the gospel, and change your church and community.

978-0-8024-1999-6 | also available as eBook and audiobook